AN ILLUSTRATED HISTORY OF
The Great Civil War

Civil War Royalists

AN ILLUSTRATED
HISTORY OF
The
Great
Civil
War

PETER YOUNG

SPURBOOKS
LIMITED

Published by Spurbooks Limited
6 Parade Court, Bourne End, Buckinghamshire

ISBN 0 904978 83 4

Designed and produced by
Mechanick Exercises, London

Typesetting by Inforum, Portsmouth
Printed in England by McCorquodale (Newton) Ltd.,
Newton-le-Willows, Lancashire.

Contents

Illustrations

6

Battle maps are by Mike Pocock

Acknowledgement is made to G.P. Bunn for permission to use photographs from his collection, and to various members of The Sealed Knot who have provided the remaining photographs used in this book.

7

Introduction

In 1642 England drifted into war: war between King Charles I and his revolted Parliament. The First Civil War went on for four years, ending with the defeat of the Royalists, but in 1648 they tried again to throw off the yoke of the Parliamentarians but in vain. Early in the following year Cromwell and Ireton arranged the trial of the King, who was later beheaded. Then followed Cromwell's Irish campaign, whose highlights were the massacres at Drogheda and Wexford, and his war with the Scots, with his victory at Dunbar (1650) and his 'crowning mercy', when he defeated King Charles II at Worcester (1651).

With the King in exile Cromwell remained in power, despite Penruddock's Rising (1655), until his death in 1658. Richard Cromwell, his son and successor had neither the inclination nor the character to rule, and no other leader emerged who could command any wide measure of support. So in 1660 a coalition of Presbyterians and Cavaliers, backed by George Monck and the English army that had been holding down Scotland, brought about the Restoration of King Charles II.

From this long struggle, emerged the system of government by which Great Britain is still ruled; but if the results of the war were largely constitutional, its causes were, in addition, religious and economic. Without all three causes it is probable that there would have been no war at all.

King Charles I had many qualities. He was a devoted husband and father, a connoisseur of the Arts, an excellent horseman, a man of great personal courage and exemplary piety. Moreover, in one of his campaigns (1644), he showed a grasp of military affairs with which he has not generally been credited. That said, it must be admitted that though serious-minded as a King, he was decidedly indifferent as a ruler, and that he had a genius for bringing trouble down upon his own head. *"The King is more willing"*, Archbishop Laud once told Strafford, *"not to hear than to hear."* Although he may have rejected good advice, like other monarchs, he had a few men of real ability among his ministers, notably Thomas Wentworth, Earl of Strafford, a formidably efficient Yorkshireman, and the little Archbishop himself. Both these men shared their ruler's authoritarian views – *"Kings are by God appointed"* – and possessed the skill to have made him as absolute a monarch as King Louis XIV was to become in France during the second half of the same century. Yet while they could have solved the problems of the day, if so permitted, the King only postponed them. For the simple truth is that the King was not industrious, particularly during the years before the War. He liked to spend his time hunting three or four times a week, in theological discussion and in the acquisition or enjoyment of works of art.

Even so, his rebellious-minded subjects could scarcely have opposed his constitutional and religious ideas had his government enjoyed a sound financial backing.

In the Middle Ages the Crown had derived most of its revenue from lands. During the previous century some of them

Infantry armed with pikes

had been sold in order to raise ready money. Much remained and rents were still considerable, though only about a third of what they had been when King James I came to the throne. Most of the Royal revenue now came from 'Tonnage and Poundage' on imported commodities, and this led to a serious quarrel in which Charles' first Parliament refused to fix the duty rate for more than a year at a time and, as C. V. Wedgewood has said:

"From the King's point of view, this was unpardonable and insulting conduct for which the laws and customs of the realm gave no authority. From the point of view of the House of Commons, it was a justifiable attempt to exert control over the royal policy, justifiable because the Commons distrusted both the policy and the advisers of the King."

This was the root of the problem – distrust.

1. Causes

When Charles I acceded to his father's throne in 1625, he inherited two deep-seated problems which were to be among the most important causes of the Civil Wars. These stumbling blocks were finance and religion and both had a history going back to the time of Elizabeth.

The Queen's death in 1603 left the Royal treasury with a deficit of £400,000. James I's efforts to restore the Royal coffers to a more healthy balance met with little success, for while he rightly stressed the necessity of maintaining adequate finances, he contrived at the same time to be a lavish and extravagant monarch, the majority of his money being spent on his favourites who were as detested by the Parliament and people as they were adored by the King. Charles I, while unlike his father in many ways, inherited this tactless attitude towards his subjects and it was to play an important part in his subsequent tussles with the Parliament which, by 1629, was in no mood to be compliant with its lord and master. Charles relied heavily on the help and support of the Duke of Buckingham (one of the most unhelpful legacies left by James I), whose presence and advice was to have disastrous consequences. Buckingham's ambitions resulted in an alliance with two Catholic countries, France and Spain; the latter being held in dislike and distrust by the majority in England where the Armada was still too recent a memory, and because of hostilities against the Protestant Netherlands. The French were meanwhile besieging the Huguenots in La Rochelle. Buckingham's reputation was not redeemed by a sudden switch of policy which resulted in the vastly expensive and utterly futile attempt to relieve La Rochelle. The assassination of the Duke in 1628 brought his counselling to an end, but the foreign policy for which he had been largely responsible, lived on. It was he who had arranged the marriage of Charles to Henrietta Maria, a French Catholic princess whose devotion to her religion disquieted more than just the ordinary citizen, whose suspicion of 'Papists' was largely founded on no more than ignorance and hearsay.

Charles' alliance with the Spanish caused an outcry, for his sister, Elizabeth, the wife of Frederick V, the Elector Palatine, was a victim of the conflict between the Protestants and Catholics. Her husband, the elected King of Bohemia, had lost his throne in 1620 and subsequent attempts to retrieve his lost kingdom proved futile. Elizabeth, the 'Winter Queen' of Bohemia, was one of England's Protestant champions. Charles' alliance with her enemies was not well received, particularly among the Puritans who had a high regard for the Queen's Calvinist husband.

Throughout the 1630s mistrust of the King's foreign policy grew both at Court, where the Queen's influence was great and Catholic proselytes were manifold, and in the country, where it seemed to ordinary folk that Charles was allying himself to the kingdom's natural enemies rather than to its friends. Charles was either unwilling or unable to take heed of his country's

Charles I with Sir Edward Waller, his Secretary-at-War

anxiety and pressed on with his design with financial, rather than political or religious goals, in mind. It was to be expected that his people, not knowing this, should misunderstand his motives or, if aware of the aim, be unsympathetic towards it.

Charles' ever-present worry was how and where to increase his revenue to cover his rising costs. Then, as now, inflation was putting up the cost of living and, as a result, the cost of all major projects undertaken by the Crown. Wars, in particular, were ruinously expensive and money had to be raised by any means which could be devised. As well as the more grandiose schemes which were contrived to enhance England's prestige abroad, more mundane pecuniary difficulties also beset the King. So unpopular was his foreign policy, however, that Parliament

14

sought to curtail those revenues which had traditionally gone to the King, the 'Tunnage and Poundage' levies. Although the King dismissed the Parliament concerned and proceeded to collect the tax himself, he was still drastically short of funds. In an effort to increase his dwindling resources, Charles looked to such antique institutions as the Court of Wards, whose old laws he revived in order to exact fines from the many who had disregarded Statutes which had not been observed for years. The rich merchants were not overlooked. Hundreds of knighthoods were bought or offered, and those who refused the honour were again fined. The revenue thus gained was useful, but it was not constant. So, in 1634 Charles introduced a new tax called Ship Money. Prior to this new tax, whenever the Navy was required to be enlarged or refurbished, the coastal towns paid a tax or actually carried out the necessary work. Charles now proposed to levy this tax throughout the kingdom. It was, on the face of it, a reasonable step to take, for England's maritime neighbours, France and the Netherlands, had growing navies and it was undesirable that England should be outstripped in sea power. Parliament did not dispute the reasoning behind the introduction of the levy, but it took issue with every other facet of the proposition it could find. For political and religious reasons, the inception of the tax was anathema to all true Parliamentarians, for since it was collected by the King for his own use, it provided him with a strong source of income without the necessity of calling a Parliament. Thus, his unpopular religious policy, as implemented by Archbishop Laud, could be put into practice unhindered. Parliament's main argument was that the King had no authority to levy such a tax directly on the people, as such an action was contrary to the powers laid down in the Petition of Right. Matters came to a head in 1637 when John Hampden, a Buckinghamshire landowner, refused to pay Ship Money to the King. In the ensuing case, Hampden lost by a narrow margin of 7 to 5, but although the King won his point, the difficulty he met with, in so doing, weakened his position to such an extent, that despite his victory, refusal to pay the tax became increasingly common.

*   *   *

In spite of this, the King's position seemed to be secure and, ruling without Parliament, he continued to uphold the 'Divine Right' as instilled into him during childhood. The next threat to his stability came not from England but from Scotland, where opposition to the attempts of first James and then his son to impose Anglican Protestantism on their unwilling subjects finally caused a crisis. In 1637, Charles I introduced a new liturgy into Scotland which was so unpopular that religious leaders drew up the National Covenant, published in 1638. Under the Covenant one of the chief bones of contention, the presence of Bishops, introduced by James, was resolved, and episcopacy was abolished. Charles cavilled at this and threatened unwisely to use force on his recalcitrant subjects. Scotland promptly raised an army to meet the menace from south of the border. This Scots force, under Alexander Leslie, a veteran of the Thirty Years War, never saw any serious action. The English threat did not materialise and Charles ended the war by the Treaty of Berwick although he regarded it more as a truce than as an end to hostilities. Thomas Wentworth, Earl of Strafford and erstwhile opponent of the King, was summoned from Ireland, where he was Lord Lieutenant, for talks with his sovereign. His change of allegiance to the side of the King was something which Parliament was never to forgive. From this time, Parliament constantly feared that any violence in England would bring Strafford across the Irish Sea with an army. On his

16

arrival at Court the Earl advised Charles to call the Parliament needed to vote money for the next Scottish expedition. This Charles did but the 'Short Parliament' as it came to be known, was more sympathetic to the Scots than to the King, and having a strong Puritan contingent, the expected support was not forthcoming. The Parliament was speedily dissolved but the second Scots war proceeded with the same consequences which had ended the first one. Most of the troops, ill-trained and badly equipped, were of Puritan persuasion and their discipline was non-existent; desertion and mutiny were rife. Communion rails, set up round altars to prevent them from being moved, were burnt by the armed rabble which finally arrived at the Border. Not surprisingly it was routed by the Scots at Newburn-on-Tyne.

*   *   *

Forced once more to treat with the Scots, Charles was the recipient of a demand for compensation. His need for money was urgent and, with the Scots now advanced as far as Newcastle, the King summoned the 'Long Parliament'. In this body, the opposition was led by John Pym, and the King's faction was markedly weaker than Pym's side. His acute shortage of money meant that Charles was unable to dissolve this dangerous Parliament and Pym, knowing this, prepared to make full use of the advantage he had thus gained. In contact with the Scots, the Parliament ensured that negotiations lasted from the middle of 1640 until September 1641 when the invaders withdrew once more. During that time great political and religious upheaval had been caused in England.

*   *   *

Parliament's first step was to confine Strafford in the Tower where Archibishop Laud shortly joined him. Although an attempt to impeach the Earl before the House of Lords failed, a Bill of Attainder was passed and Charles, hoping that his signature to the document would satisfy the dissenters in Parliament, signed it and so authorised Strafford's execution. This was but a beginning however, for now Parliament passed the Triennial Act, stating that Parliament had to meet at least every three years with or without the summons of the Crown. Prerogative courts – including the Star Chamber which had been responsible for passing sentences of mutilation on William Prynne – were abolished, as were all non-Parliamentary taxes, a measure which encompassed the fateful Ship Money levy. Charles assented to all these measures on the same day that he signed Strafford's Bill of Attainder.

Religious differences remained however, and the other Parliamentary reforms having been won so easily, caused the extremists to now come forward, pulling behind them the moderates who sought to mitigate the radicals' effect. It was generally felt that the Church as well as the State should be brought within Parliamentary control, but the introduction of the Root and Branch Bill in 1641, seeking to abolish episcopacy and the Book of Common Prayer, went too far for the moderates whose alternative Bill on Church reform did not put an end to episcopacy, but sought instead to strip the bishops of their temporal powers and to force them to preach regularly.

All this was achieved while the end of the Second Bishop's War with Scotland was being negotiated. After the Treaty of Ripon concluded hostilities with the Scots, an outbreak of violence in Ulster posed an even greater threat to the frail stability between King and Parliament. With the removal of Strafford, power in Ireland passed to the Puritan Lords who epitomised to the Irish the Englishmen who had taken over their lands and forced alien laws upon them. In the Catholic rising which followed, hundreds of Protestants were killed and tales of atrocities, magnified in the telling, seriously alarmed the English. Suspicion of Royal complicity grew when forged Royal Commissions were found in the rebel's possession, so that when it was proposed that an army be sent to crush the rising, no Royal nominee to head the force was considered. It was Oliver Cromwell who proposed that Essex should be appointed by Parliament to crush the Irish rebellion. Meanwhile Pym demanded that the King should remove all his 'evil' counsellors, and that they should be replaced by those approved by Parliament. Until this was done, Charles would get no assistance from Parliament in solving the nation's problems in Ireland.

Parliament had, in effect, made a bid to control not only the militia but also the Ministers traditionally appointed by the King. They went even further; just before the King returned to his capital in November 1641, after the conclusion of the Scots war, Parliament passed the 'Grand Remonstrance', which criticised in detail all Charles' contentious actions from the time of his accession. It was the work of extremists who were themselves divided, but after a hot debate, it was passed by a majority of eleven. Charles might have been expected to provide a reply to this document, thus giving further opportunity for attack on the monarch's mode of rule. On his return to London, however, Charles showed no disposition to take any notice of the document and, after a welcome by the Royalist mayor, he retired to Hampton Court with his family. By now unrest had spread beyond the confines of the Court and Commons and street fighting was breaking out in London. At Hampton Court, Charles received a deputation from the Commons asking him to consider the Remonstrance. Charles agreed and asked that the document should not meanwhile be published. Meanwhile the King removed Essex from his post as Commander-in-Chief and

A mixture of arms, cannon, pike and musket

removed the London Trained Bands from their position of
guarding the Palace of Westminster, placing Royalist halber-
diers under the Earl of Dorset there instead. It was this body
which broke up the 'No Popery' demonstration outside the
Commons on the 29th November. The Commons next received
a petition asking that the control of the militia should be taken
from the King. When the Militia Bill was passed by 158 votes to
125, Charles replied that he would only assent to it if his rights
were respected, that is the traditional rights of the English
monarchy and the Church of England. It was evident that
Parliament would not agree to this and the Bill was not signed

by the King but passed as an Ordinance. Nevertheless, it was regarded as legal by Londoners and neighbouring counties. Charles, annoyed that the Remonstrance had been printed and distributed against his wishes, rejected it on the 23rd December.

*   *   *

While Pym's agents promoted alarm at Court by spreading rumours that Parliament intended to impeach the Queen, the City of London was in a tumult as people gathered to prevent the bishops taking their seats in the House of Lords. Threats of violence were as yet one-sided, for the King was unable to make a real show of force. He knew that Parliament could and would withold 'Tunnage and Poundage' in the event of strife, a move which could bankrupt him. These two considerations were taken into account, but the King still decided to act and ordered the arrest of Lord Mandeville and five MPs – Pym, John Hampden, Denzil Holles, Sir Arthur Hesilrige and William Strode. The Lords, while sympathising with the King, did not grant the Order which they felt would jeopardise their own position. They declined to acknowledge the King's right to impeach. Charles then took the matter into his own hands and went to the House of Commons himself with the Warrant. Warned by Lucy Carlisle, one of Pym's spies and one of the Queen's ladies-in-waiting, the Members had fled into hiding 'and Charles, out-manoeuvred, retired once more to Hampton Court leaving London in the hands of the Parliament. The next time he was to enter his capital it was as a prisoner. While the extremism of the Parliament gained him the support of such moderate men as Hyde, Falkland and Digby, the King was still in a weak position. His volatile wife tended to support any means by which power

21

could be restored to the Crown, and these included violence. The 'Army Plot' was hatched and supported by the Queen. The two conflicting options, capitulation or war, left the King, as usual, undecided as to the best course of action. The compromise he chose was of all the options open to him the least satisfactory. Following the moderates' line, he continued negotiations with Pym, but with little intention of settling the dispute. He was already planning for the inevitable with his more martial advisers, thus ensuring that the rift would widen into armed conflict. The absence of the moderates from Westminster hardened the attitude of those left there and as the King journeyed to York in June 1642, the Commons drew up nineteen propositions which followed Charles north. The time for talking was over however, for already the Queen had gone abroad, not only ostensibly to attend her daughter's wedding to the Dutch Prince William, but also to pawn the Crown Jewels in order to raise money for an army. The Commons, gaining control of the fleet, appointed the Earl of Warwick as commander of the Navy while Essex was made commander of the Army once again. Charles secured Newcastle and issued Commissions of Array from York. Both sides were now committed to finding arms and money for a fight which was to last a decade and fundamentally alter the English constitution.

2. Assets

'Moneys are the nerves of war'

KING CHARLES I

Outside the metropolis, where the pace of life was more leisurely and news was apt to travel slowly, there was less inclination to become involved in the quarrel between Charles and his Parliament. There had been constitutional upheavals before, when in 1629 the King had embarked on a period of personal rule which lasted eleven years, and the country gentry, whose interests were often more agrarian than political, undoubtedly felt that now, as before, the quarrel would eventually blow over. Even when it became increasingly evident that the actions of the protagonists would lead to war, those conservative and peace-loving burghers and landowners did their utmost to remain firmly seated on the fence.

A considerable proportion of the male population of England never actually took up arms in the war, but it soon became very difficult for the prominent provincial squires to remain neutral. If they did not go to war, the war tended to come to them. As the two sides began to raise and equip armies, money, men and supplies were sought, and the hunt for all three gradually penetrated even the most insignificant of hamlets. Even if the gentry in the area were uncommitted to either side, the descent of officers and quartermasters in search of men, supplies, horses or billets often led to tacit, if not willing, co-operation with whichever side happened to be there.

It was already clear, however, that the conflict was by no means a social one, neither was it economic in character, nor yet, strangely, religious or political, although most Puritans espoused the cause of the Parliament and most Arminians that of the King. Politically, the so-called 'ruling classes' were split arbitrarily and the result was that although the majority of the House of Commons did not support the King, a significant minority did. The greater part of the Lords was Royalist, but with significant abstentions. The reasons for this division were more emotional than rational. It has already been noted that the extremism of Pym and his followers in forcing the Grand Remonstrance through Parliament alienated many of his former supporters and drove them to the King's side. The King might in the same way be said to have forced many peers, for small or personal reasons, to support the Parliament. Many may have felt piqued because they were not given the lucrative court positions they had coveted; others undoubtedly felt that the King's recent policy of selling titles in order to bolster his dwindling resources cheapened the peerage; and if the King had felt confident that these newly-created noblemen would support him if only out of gratitude, he was sadly mistaken.

Many men had a difficult choice to make and the fact that conviction often split families and parted friends is evidence of a thin dividing line. Sir Edmund Verney, a Puritan who held a court appointment, could not find it in him to desert the monarch he had served for so long, although they were religiously deeply different. Of Verney's three sons, one fought for

24

John Pym

Parliament and the other two for the King. Sir William Waller and Ralph Hopton, lifelong friends, were destined to meet on opposite sides at several battle-fields, although both were Puritans and sincerely religious, with no initial desire to fight at all. If religion and politics were not the deciding factors as to which side a man supported, economics surely played its part, particularly in the provinces, although again this was not an absolute factor any more than the others were. London, the social, political and economic hub of the kingdom was Parliamentarian in outlook and the urban centres elsewhere in the land tended to follow in the wake of the capital, though this was by no means a universal phenomenon, and some cities, such as Bristol, were forced to declare for the Parliament, despite the fact that there

25

was a strong Royalist party within them. The tendency for the more industrially advanced centres to be against the King may be explained by the fact that both James and Charles had indulged in the unpopular pastime of selling monopolies to rich merchants, who thus acquired a stronghold over whichever branch of the trade they were engaged in. This practice had enriched many merchants and impoverished others, and while the obvious resultant allegiance to either the King or Parliament applied in most cases, it was not always in evidence.

Having established their allegiance, the main cities hastened to secure what arms they could. In some towns, weapons for the militia were seized, while in others, notably in the north where the Scots Wars had resulted in a supply of more modern arms than those generally kept for local Trained Bands, large amounts of stores were simply appropriated. By the very nature of things, Parliament greatly benefited from these arsenals and as most sea ports and the majority of the Navy were disaffected from the King, the Royalists had initially little of the paraphernalia of war with which to equip themselves.

England had enjoyed peace at home for more than 100 years and the vigilance of the local militia which had been well drilled during the reign of Elizabeth generally died out during the time of James and Charles. The potential for an army seemed to be very limited; the two wars in which England became involved under the aegis of the Duke of Buckingham had done nothing whatever for England's reputation abroad and augured badly for the military minds faced with the task of raising the opposing armies in 1642. However, if there had been no wars in which the English were directly involved on the continent, there were plenty of armies fighting each other within Europe itself. It was in such fields as these that a few Englishmen had learned the art of war in the service of Holland, France, Spain or Sweden. Little knowledge indeed had been gleaned from Buckingham's fruitless efforts and still less from the ignominious Scots wars. The few English regiments thus employed provided a nucleus of suitable men on which to build the English armies. These professional soldiers were much sought after by both sides and inducements were offered in order to secure the allegiance of the mercenaries. Although some officers were thus recruited into the embryonic forces, there was still the problem of obtaining the soldiers to carry out their commands. There was no army in existence in England; defence was left to those groups of local militia known as the Trained Bands, whose field of activity was confined to stated boundaries beyond which they were not compelled to move. In the main these forces were of indifferent quality, poorly and infrequently drilled, with old weapons which were usually kept rusting away in the town magazine. There were two notable exceptions to this generalisation and these were the Trained Bands of London and Cornwall. The latter were pugnacious and tough but refused initially to cross the Tamar into what they regarded as 'foreign' territory. The London Trained Bands, under the command of Philip Skippon, were at the disposal of Essex for Parliament numbering about 6,000. They were thus a useful force, particularly as on occasion they would move beyond their prescribed boundaries to fight. Once again, as urban centres tended to declare for the Parliament, the Trained Bands' magazines fell into the hands of the Parliament, which deprived the Royalists of yet another source of arms. The rich merchants of London also gave considerable financial support to Parliament which thus, with more weapons and strong financial backing, began the war with an advantage over the Royalists who relied for their funds on those relatively few wealthy men who recruited and equipped their own forces at their own expense. At the outbreak of hostilities the Parliament, with the equipment from all the main arsenals of the kingdom, and a substantial amount of arms from the magazines

27

of the Trained Bands, had therefore the upper hand on two counts. The Royalists, on the other hand, were forced to rely on several different sources for their arms. Like the Roundheads, they looked to the Trained Band magazines and to those arms stores which could be found in the loyal towns and universities – notably, of course, Oxford – but the two great arsenals of the Tower and Hull were irreplaceable losses. The purchase of equipment on the Continent was vital, but transportation to England was a risky undertaking, although the Dutch Stadtholder, Frederick Henry, whose son, William, had married Charles' eldest daughter, Mary, at the beginning of 1642, not only afforded Henrietta Maria hospitality after she had pawned the English Crown Jewels to raise money for men and arms, but

A skirmish line of musketeers protects the cannon

also provided naval escorts for Royalist merchandise. Within England, several Royalists were able to provide a considerable quantity of arms and armour to equip troops of men, and some noblemen even had small pieces of artillery at their disposal. When even the most obsolete and almost unserviceable equipment was resurrected from various barns, attics, storerooms and cellars in which it had been mouldering, the Royalist army was still sadly lacking in arms and armour. There was only one course of action left to them, and that was to improvise their weapons and therefore, to some extent, their tactics. When, at last, the Royalists began to move south from York, the King summoned the Trained Bands in towns on the way, recruiting those willing to follow him and taking the weapons of the others to augment his own meagre resources.

Perhaps the most important source of supply in the early stages of the war was the capture of equipment from the Roundheads. The early successes which the Royalists gained brought with them captured arms and ammunition without which certain elements of the Royalist force would probably have disintergrated. Despite the fecundity displayed by Royalist quartermasters, however, the army was still under-equipped by the time Edgehill, the first great pitched battle of the war, was fought in October.

In spite of the disparity in the armies, both were organised by a handful of professional soldiers and a number of amateurs whose enthusiasm was often more political or religious than military. The opposing sides evolved similarly and fought using tactics which varied only slightly, employing a mixture of traditional English military organisation and the methods of warfare learned on the Continent, chiefly from the Dutch princes Henry and Maurice and the Swedish king Gustavus Adolphus.

3. The Art of War in the 17th Century

Because the armies raised in England during 1642 included a few professional soldiers, the tactics instilled into the men owed something to the Continental schools of warfare in which those men had learned their skills. The vast majority of both officers and men were military neophytes, and the slight knowledge they possessed was generally confined to and derived from the limits of tradition and verbal communication on the subject of the military art, both of which fell far short of actual experience.

European warfare had seen the gradual decline in the effectiveness of cavalry, which had been so prevalent in the Middle Ages. The development of the long bow, and later of firearms, checked the rise of the heavily armoured horseman, whose early impact had been made chiefly through the infantry's initial inability to withstand the advance of impregnable, mounted swordsmen. More important in the decline of horse was the rise of disciplined foot – in particular the Swiss pikemen – who formed defensive squares or 'hedgehogs' which consisted of a mass of men who opposed and successfully repulsed the onslaught of cavalry. In formation, the 'hedgehog' probably owed something to the Roman *testudo* although the latter was to guard against artillery rather than cavalry charges.

With these main causes, the cavalry had declined by the end of the 16th century to a role equal, if not subordinate, to that played by the infantry. Indeed, the role of shock tactics was transferred from the cavalry to the infantry and the cavalry was reduced to playing a part which was little more than that of mounted infantry, that is to say, the horseman, equipped with a wheel-lock pistol, advanced on the foot and paused before giving fire and returning to the rear of the formation. This manoeuvre, known as the *caracole*, had several disadvantages. Firstly the musket, which was now being developed, was used in the 'hedgehog' interspersed with pikes, and as its range was greater than that of the wheellock pistol, the cavalry was very vulnerable as it approached the infantry. Secondly, consideration had to be given to the horse itself which was increasingly reluctant to face the lethal groups of infantry in which the essentially vulnerable musketeers were protected by the pikemen, thus presenting a formidable array. Finally, the cavalryman himself was presented with a problem, in that the introduction of firearms to the cavalry created great difficulty, for it is not at all easy to give steady accurate fire from a moving platform.

Following the decline of the cavalry, the development of new infantry techniques to provide the shock tactics needed, became vital. The problem was allied to that of the role of cavalry which had become of secondary importance. Infantry, on the other hand, was developing into a more complex arm in which a combination of firepower and shock tactics were employed. The solutions to the problems of deployment of the various types of foot soldier, and the strength in which each was used, varied from country to country. The Spaniards, in introducing the '*tercio*' formation, provided one answer to the problem. The 'tercio' consisted of a mass of pikemen, surrounded by musketeers, in total numbering, as the name implies, about 3,000 men. Firepower and shock tactics were thus combined, but the formation was large and unwieldly and as a result, immobile. A further problem was that the many mercenaries fighting on the Continent at the turn of the 17th century were reluctant to engage in conclusive actions for the obvious reason that decisive battles tended to curtail wars and thus render the soldiers unemployed. The new style of infantry formation had, as one of its chief aims, the quicker despatch of the enemy and it was thus difficult to persuade the mercenaries to use it.

It was not long before refinements to this form of deployment were introduced. The Dutch Prince, Maurice, made use of a smaller unit, the 'battalion', which was shallower and less dense in formation and, although inflexible in use, made better use of man power. These two methods of deployment were extensively used on the Continent with some success despite the mercenaries' continuing resistance to the conclusive actions desired by the politicians. The Swedish soldier King, Gustavus Adolphus, made extensive modifications to the methods in use at the outbreak of the Thirty Years' War. Where Maurice's battalions had been ten ranks in depth, Gustavus reduced the number to six. Finding, in addition, that the method of giving fire by countermarch was slow and wasteful, the King further lessened the number of ranks to three and also introduced the method of firing by salvo in which all ranks fired at once, leaving the pikemen to advance on the disordered enemy during reloading. Three or four of these 'battalions' made up the Swedish *brigade* which usually formed into a wedge-shape and was augmented by the addition of a small regimental gun, normally of no higher calibre than a *drake* or *saker*, which greatly enhanced the firing power of the body. It was not to infantry alone, however, that Gustavus confined his innova-

32

A company of musketeers

tions. Cavalry underwent equally fundamental changes of style, changes which included the abandonment of the *caracole* and the somewhat pedestrian style of the mounted arm. The re-introduction of the cavalry charge meant that the great mass of horse needed to perform the *caracole* was reduced to a mere six ranks or even, on occasion, to three. Unlike the Dutch, the Swedes did not pause to give fire before engaging their opponents, but waited until they were actually among the enemy before discharging their weapons. Cavalry against cavalry found this new speed and style effective, but it was still not possible for the faster horse to attack and break up a determined and disciplined body of foot. Gustavus tried to solve this problem by attempting first to shake the foot before sending the horse in. This was done by interspersing his bodies of horse with musketeers who gave fire as the horse advanced. The unfortunate musketeer, however, hampered by a great deal of unwieldly equipment, was scarcely mobile enough to move with

Push of Pike

the cavalry, but the firepower they provided before the charge was certainly of use to the cavalry, since their own firepower was retained unimpaired until after the initial shock. It was on the field of Breitenfeld that the superiority of these tactics was demonstrated when, on the 17th September 1631, Pappenheim and Tilly were defeated by Gustavus Adolphus.

34

Not unexpectedly, most of the mercenaries employed by either King or Parliament, took on the role of military adviser and each had his own preference as to which mode of warfare was most effective. The chief schools of thought divided into two camps, the Dutch and the Swedish. There were, however, various factors inherent in the situation which meant that no single, unadulterated method of fighting survived the melting pot into which it was thrown, as the English commanders, experienced or otherwise, began to marshal their forces. If it was not sheer topographical problems which precluded the use of tactics proved successful on the continent, it was some more mundane consideration, such as the lack of arms or the inability to train the eager but callow recruits.

*   *   *

There had been no serious battle on English soil since Bosworth Field in 1485, and the terrain over which that action had been fought, while not dissimilar to that of England in the 1640's, nevertheless presented fresh problems to the 17th century armies, which had not bothered their 15th century counterparts. The country was less enclosed than it is today, making favourable ground for cavalry to charge on. The exceptions to this were few, but Newbury provides one example, for there the enclosures seriously hampered the horse while giving the foot ample cover for defensive positions. Communications were bad and roads were often impassable to all but horsemen and could be expected to hold up the progress of any fully equipped army which included numerous baggage wagons. As an alternative, supplies were often sent by water; the Parliament held most English ports and had the advantage of the use of the coastal waters, but both sides made use of rivers wherever possible.

There was little industry in 17th-century England and towns

tended to be small, walled, and isolated. Often they possessed remains of a medieval defence system, usually in an unusable state, rotted by years of neglect and frequently beyond repair, as for example the defences of Worcester. For strategic purposes, the number of outmoded but still strong stone fortresses which owed their existence to the baronial wars of forgotten ancestors, were of more use. These edifices, though an offence to the eye of the military purist of the time, were not difficult to defend and presented grave difficulties to those who sought to capture them. Despite the rapid development of more effective siege artillery, this equipment was in fairly short supply throughout the Civil War and such fortresses could and did block the rapid advance of armies for a considerable time while the necessary process of reduction was undertaken. Basing House is a particularly good example of this activity. Town defences, also subjected to the rigours of onslaught by siege artillery, were often more easy prey since the crumbling defences were widely dispersed and often bolstered up by earthworks designed to repulse infantry assault rather than a battery of siege guns. Soldiers' weapons of the period were primitive and, as far as firearms were concerned, often unreliable. In the infantry, there were three types of weapon; the matchlock and flintlock muskets and the pike. Of the muskets, the matchlock was more common, flintlocks being used chiefly to guard artillery trains where a lighted match constituted an obvious danger in the presence of gunpowder. The musketeer, while wearing no armour, was hampered by the great amount of ancillary equipment required for the use of his weapon. Firstly, he carried a bandolier, attached to which were twelve (usually) small cartridges containing one charge of black powder. These cartridges were known, inevitably, as the 'apostles'. In addition, there was a pouch containing wadding and bullets and a flask containing the fine powder used for priming the pan. Muskets

36

were nearly five feet long and had to be fired with the barrel placed on a *rest* – a stick with a pointed end and forked top into which the musket was laid. The *rest* was a cumbersome, if necessary, piece of equipment which did nothing but complicate the drill to which the musketeer was subjected. Finally, the musketeer was issued with a length of *match* – cord soaked in saltpetre – which was kept alight at both ends and held in the left hand. This hazardous piece of equipment caused a considerable number of accidents during battle when, in the heat of the moment, a soldier inadvertently put his left hand into the powder barrel to replenish his supply of charges! The loss of his left hand, if not of the powder monkey, was the invariable result.

The procedure for loading a musket – *casting about* – was a long and tedious one and when complete the weapon could only be relied upon to be accurate up to a distance of 40 yards. On average, a musketeer could not fire more than two rounds a minute and there was always the risk of a *flash in the pan*, in which case, the musketeer had either to pray that he fired successfully at the next attempt or had to spend a great deal of time cleaning powder, wadding and bullet out of his weapon. These muzzle-loading weapons were difficult enough to load in ordinary conditions, while in wet weather, the task became even harder, for not only did the ammunition have to be kept dry, but the match had also to be kept alight. On long manoeuvres, the problems of burning match in enormous, wasteful quantities were manifest; at night, musketeers on the march provided small, glowing targets for their enemies to aim at. It is small wonder that the musketeer, with his cumbersome and unreliable weapon, was not granted a very high status by his fellow soldiers.

The pikeman, on the other hand, was considered to be the more important of the two types of foot soldier and more prestige was attached to him. The pike itself was a simple weapon, consisting of a long pole of anything between twelve and eighteen feet to which a metal head was attached. The strongest men were chosen to wield the pike, for not only was the weapon difficult to handle safely and effectively, but the men were also equipped with heavy armour to protect them from cavalry attack. Usually a set of armour comprised a back and breast plate, a gorget which was worn to protect the throat, steel thigh guards and a helmet, which was known as the 'pot'. All ranks, in theory, carried a short sword. Officers in the foot carried a *partisan* to distinguish them from Sergeants, whose weapon was a *halberd*.

* * *

Of the three or four types of horse which had flourished during the 16th century, most had become obsolete by the outbreak of the Civil War. Cuirassiers and lancers were no longer in use, because their very heavy armour was insupportable both for the wearer and the bearer. The light horse which was most prevalent on both sides during the war, was equipped with a carbine, a pair of pistols and a sword. Horse firearms could not, for obvious reasons, use the matchlock ignition system. Instead, wheel-lock or flintlocks were used. The former consisted of a wheel with a serrated edge against which a piece of pyrites was held. The wheel was wound up – or *spauned* – and when the trigger was pulled, the spring holding the wheel was released and the pyrites created sparks which passed through the touch hole and ignited the powder. Unfortunately, if the wheel was *spauned* any length of time before it was used, the pistol was liable to misfire, i.e. the wheel did not rotate because the spring became stuck.

A variety of other weapons and armour was used, particularly by the Royalists who suffered a shortage of equipment more than that of the Roundheads. Fowling pieces were often

38

used, indicative of the shortage of firearms. So chronic was this to begin with that often only the first two or three ranks of horse were equipped with any sort of firearm and the rest of the force had to rely on swords. There were several types of sword in use; the thin bladed rapier, which was part of the ordinary dress of any gentleman was one of the most common types, the military version of the rapier, the *Poppenheimer*, was also popular, but these weapons were for thrusting and less useful in a *melee* than the 'cut and thrust' types of which the *walloon* sword and basket-hilt *mortuary* sword were the most used.

Cavalrymen on both sides wore armour at the beginning of the War, but few people were still wearing it by the time the War ended. The buff coat was universally worn, however, throughout the war. This was a leather jerkin which gave protection to mid-thigh length and often had sleeves as well. The garment gave protection against sword cuts while giving the horseman a lot more mobility than he would have enjoyed in armour. Like pikemen, the trooper wore a 'back and breast' or corselet, and a pot helmet. There were two types of pot, the Dutch pot, with a single noseguard, and the English *lobster* pot with three face guards. Less common were gorgets and steel gauntlets, although these were worn, particularly by the officers who probably found it easier to come by these scarce items.

In a class of their own were the *dragoons*, a type of mounted infantry, slower moving than the horse, yet more manoeuvrable than the foot. They owed their name to the weapon which they had originally carried, the *dragon*, a musket-bored carbine. Dragoons often fought dismounted, flanking battlefields and holding outposts, armed with a musket and sword, although the former was slung on a belt like cavalry carbines. No armour was worn, often not even a buff coat. Dragoons, with cheaper horses, arms and armour, were probably the most inexpensive branch of the army.

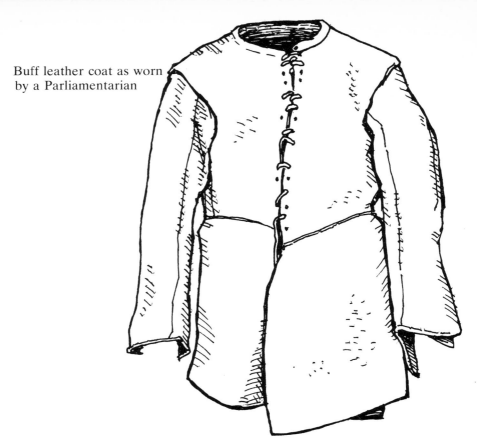

Buff leather coat as worn
by a Parliamentarian

Although soldiers did not wear uniforms of anything like the correct precision demanded by military tailors today, they were certainly provided with some clothing – the amount varied according to the inclination and the degree of solvency of the Regimental commander, at least until the inception of the New Model Army. Within companies, if not Regiments, there was an attempt to conform, if only in the colour of the coats worn. Hence it was usually possible to identify a regiment by the colour it sported; Prince Rupert's bluecoats, Newcastle's whitecoats, Broughton's greencoats, and so on. Both sides had several red-blue-green or purple-coated regiments and confusion was inevitable. Generally speaking, officers and sergeants did not wear uniform at all and were thus distinguishable from

40

their men. Only on the Roundhead side was any attempt made to differentiate between regiments and ranks and this was done by issuing coats with different coloured linings – the origin of the later regimental facings. In general, the items most commonly issued to soldiers were: double breeches, stockings, shoes (or boots) and headwear, although cloaks or cassocks were sometimes included.

After the raising of the New Model Army, the Roundhead army, all dressed in red, presented a very different aspect from that of the Royalists whose Army by 1645 had been so decimated that it had to amalgamate several regiments, and therefore presented a motley spectacle by comparison.

Headgear was also an item which lent unity to a regiment. Pikemen, musketeers and cavalry on both sides favoured the same type of hat or helmet; pikemen wore a steel helmet with a ridge running from front to back and a rim which rose to a point on the forehead and protected the back of the neck to some extent. Musketeers usually wore wide-brimmed felt hats or beavers, more often than not sporting feathers; cavalrymen wore helmets or monteros. The *Monmouth cap* was also worn by the infantry, although not in battle. This appears to have been a knitted, tasselled concoction but no examples survive, so its appearance must be left to conjecture.

Footwear was an item of general issue and therefore tended to be uniform. Infantry wore low shoes, tied over the instep. Though light, they must have been difficult to keep on during the rigours of a long march and it is doubtful that they were waterproof. Cavalry boots, on the other hand, were more substantial, reaching to the thighs and being rendered water-proof by the application of a tallow beeswax mixture. Such were the degrees of uniformity that confusion between the sides in battle was not uncommon and further precautions had to be taken in order that this did not happen. Sashes were worn by the two

Army in Review – from a 17th century print by Jacques Callot

armies. The Royalists wore red or pink, the Roundheads orange. As a further precaution, field signs were adopted so that, for example, at the storming of Bristol, the Royalists fought without collars. The two sides were also able to identify each other by the field slogans or battle cries which were used during battle. At Marston Moor the Roundheads shouted '*God with us*', while the Royalists gave vent to '*God and King*'. Despite these ruses, however, it was still possible either to mistake the regiment or to circumvent the enemy and escape capture.

Both horse and foot in the Royalist and Parliamentarian armies were organised into regiments, although the size of this unit varied in the armies according to the wishes of the High Command and the availability of recruits. A Royalist cavalry regiment, in theory, numbered 500 men and was divided into six troops which were commanded by three field officers, colonel, lieutenant-colonel and major, and three captains. In practice, however, the six troops were rarely up to strength, being closer to a total of 70 men per troop. A regiment had, besides its field officers and troop commanders, three other officers, a lieutenant, a cornet and a quartermaster.

Roundhead regiments were organised differently, having only two field officers, a colonel and a major. Unlike the Royalists their normal troop complement was 71 men and this total was often exceeded. The Royalists had an initial advantage in that most of the country gentry followed the King and these men, having ridden from childhood, were much more suited to cavalry than were the recruits of the Parliament. The Royalists needed to be better horsemen, for the Roundheads had the better weapons and had no need to use their horses as instruments of attack in the way that the Royalists did. Thus the Roundheads generally fought after the Dutch fashion, using their mounts more as a firing platform, discharging their pistols before engaging, while the Royalists, under the aegis of Prince Rupert, held their fire until after they had charged at speed, and engaged. At the beginning of the war, however, these capable horsemen, totally lacking military experience, suffered from a lack of discipline, and once they had charged – which they undoubtedly did with valour – they lacked the control to stop, turn and reform. It was left to the New Model Army to instil into its soldiers the discipline necessary to charge and to follow up the charge; an important development since it was often at that stage that the battle was won or lost.

*   *   *

Infantry Regiments consisted of ten companies, commanded by three field officers, as with the cavalry, and seven captains. A regiment, with its full complement of men had 200 men in the colonel's company, 160 in the lieutenant-colonel's, 140 in the major's and 100 in the rest. Each company also had a lieutenant, an ensign, two sergeants, three corporals and a drummer. Unlike the cavalry, this arm of the force possessed rudimentary medical facilities, each regiment having a surgeon and a surgeon's mate although these men could do little in a battle where casualties were heavy. In the cavalry, the farrier usually performed the duties of a surgeon. In theory an infantry company (and regiment) consisted of two-thirds musketeers and one-third pikemen, although this balance was not always applied. The company was presented six ranks deep in battle, each rank with a file leader whose second-in-command brought up the rear. It could not be expected that the inexperienced levies would become proficient in the complicated infantry drill all at once. Musketeers had their procedure simplified in firing by introduction or extraduction when ranks fired in turn, following which rear ranks moved forward and front ranks moved to the rear. Firing by salvo became more common as the war progressed, the ranks of musketeers being reduced to three for the purpose.

In battle, the regiment was drawn up with pike in the centre, flanked by musketeers although the pikes could divide into two bodies, each flanked by musketeers, thus forming two wings and so extending the line. In battle, the infantry's first move was to fire on the enemy, following which the pikemen went in to engage the enemy. In this they were often helped by the musketeers whose weapons were heavy enough to provide an effective cudgel. Attacked by cavalry, the regiment formed a circle with pikemen, drummer and colour on the inside, the musketeers on the outside. In this event, musketeers were sometimes provided with *swines-feathers*, sharpened stakes which were planted to protect them from the marauding cavalry. These served to perform the function of pikes; it was not until the invention of the bayonet that the pike was superseded.

Infantry and cavalry of both sides used the same system of

44

colours and each company had its own colour, guidon or standard. Company colours indicated the status of its commander, so that for example, a colonel's colour was plain while a lieutenant-colonel's colour had a small St. George's Cross in the left-hand corner nearest the colour staff. Captain's colours were the most ornamental and devices were often derived from the armorial bearings of the colonel, although on the Roundhead side colours tended to be biblical in their origin. Dragoons and cavalry had smaller colours for ease of carrying on horseback.

Artillery during the Civil War was looked upon by all but the *cognoscienti* as a science with a great deal of mystique attached to it. There were ten types of gun in use during the war although the definitions between them were not always clear and calibres were often confused. The greatest number of guns was of the middle calibre, ranging from *Culverins* to *Falcons*, although others were in use. The high calibre cannon were not so frequently employed because they were cumbersome to transport and difficult to site. In battle, the field-pieces were generally placed between regiments of foot while, if any large calibre pieces were present, they were placed, if possible, on high ground behind the battlefield, although this practice presupposed that both armies would remain more or less where they were and therefore not disturb the range of the artillery. Most infantry regiments on both sides had one or two light pieces of the calibre of a *drake* or *saker* to increase their firepower, following the Swedish example.

Loading an artillery piece by the muzzle was, as with a musket, a crude and often dangerous business, although the risk here was greater since the quantities of powder were obviously bigger than with small arms. Roundshot was most often used although case shot was also employed, usually against close range infantry, since a canister of musket balls spraying from the muzzle of the gun was most effective.

There was a lamentable lack of supplies and transport to

begin with in both armies. There was an allowance laid down for each soldier in respect of food and drink, but often this was not available and the men were allowed to live at free quarter. Fast moving horse, often a long way from the body of the army, also lived in this way when other sources of supply ran out, which they usually did. 'Free-quarter' was, naturally, unpopular with the people on whom it was inflicted, although they were provided with tickets which in theory were redeemable for cash at the local headquarters. It was a system which all too often failed to work. Both armies attempted to provide central food stores and sources of production, but distribution to widely scattered forces meant that, all too often, 'free-quarter' was inflicted on the luckless populace. To these disadvantages may be added the obvious military disadvantage that 'free-quarter' scattered troops and eroded discipline, making troops easy prey for the marauding enemy.

Although, in theory, pay for a soldier was constant, neither officers nor men were regularly reimbursed for their pains, even in the New Model Army where in 1644 the officers were put on half pay, the other half to be made up to them after the end of the War.

With the fluctuating fortunes of the treasuries, the only other inducement which prompted a soldier to enlist was the prospect of plunder. Prisoners-of-war were deprived of arms, equipment and horse which were swiftly disposed of within the ranks of the victors.

Towns having the misfortune to be taken by storm were considered ripe for pillage and a specific time was laid aside for this ceremony to be performed. Civil dignitaries often found it sound economics to negotiate a cash payment in lieu of pillage. Another means of avoiding this wasteful and costly pastime was for the assaulting commanders to give their troops *storm-money* in lieu of plunder.

Although both sides recruited widely in England, there remained many areas only slightly informed of the true state of affairs, and at the outbreak of the war there were still many people who had no idea of the true state of the nation. Those, however, who did know were initially willing recruits and voluntary enlistment was all that was needed. This was particularly true on large estates where tenants were usually quite happy to follow the cause of their master. Cornwall and Wales were fruitful areas for the recruitment of Royalist foot while the south-east and East Anglia provided the Roundheads with many of their men.

As the war progressed, however, irregular pay and other difficulties led to widespread desertion, in particular among conscripted or pressed men of whom there became an increasing number as the war rolled on. It is likely that most of the population was eventually involved with the war in one way or another; those who did not fight were probably subjected to pillage or the recipients of requests from men for free-quarter.

*   *   *

The command structure of both armies was similar. A Captain-General headed the army and he was assisted by a staff which represented all sections of his force, as well as his lieutenant-general and field-marshal. Horse, foot and artillery all had generals at their head, seconded by lieutenant-generals. Below these ranks, the foot had a Sergeant-Major-General and the horse a Commissary-General. These men were often of greater military experience than their two superior officers and acted as advisers to them. Unfortunately, the intrusion of social and political considerations meant that these posts were often either left unfilled or one man filled more than one post, thus snaring up the chain of command and leading to confusion. The Council of War further complicated the situation. This body, consisting of civilians and soldiers, met to decide strategy and tactics, but more often tore itself asunder with internal strife caused by conflicting interests.

In the Royalist Army, the King held the rank of Captain-General and his staff was, for all practical purposes, his Council of War whose composition varied from time to time throughout the conflict. The high command varied little, however, and was initially headed by Lord Lindsey as Lord General. Lindsey was mortally wounded at Edgehill and was replaced by Patrick Ruthven, Lord Forth. The post of General of the Horse was held by Charles' nephew, Prince Rupert, whose deputy was Lord Henry Wilmot. Sir Jacob Astley was Sergeant-Major-General of the Foot and exercised practical control over that arm of the force. Sir Arthur Aston commanded the Dragoons

Statue of Charles I, Whitehall

and Sir John Heydon the Artillery. The Parliamentarian structure was less decisive and had no real head, unlike the Royalists, who in theory, at least, had the King. Robert Devereux, the Earl of Essex, was Captain-General of the Force whose Horse was commanded by the Earl of Bedford, seconded by his Lieutenant-General, Sir William Balfour. The command of the Foot changed several times, beginning with Colonel Thomas Ballard and passing to Philip Skippon and Sir John Merrick. The General of the Ordnance was the Earl of Peterborough, his Lieutenant-General being Philibert Emanuel Du Bois. Other officers held prestigious staff appointments for no apparent reason other than the probable one that influence was brought to bear to gain the coveted post of aide-de-camp or adjutant.

In the field, command above regimental level was not permanent. *Tertio* commanders varied from campaign to campaign and even the *tertio* itself rarely comprised the same regiment from one battle to the next. It was on the *tertio* commander that the onus of action rested in battle, for Generals usually commanded from behind the army, on horseback or even in a carriage. In the middle of 1642, there was still a strong body of opinion in both camps, which advocated negotiation, but they were too late. The embryonic and inexperienced armies were drawing ever closer to bloodshed.

4. The Campaign of 1642

The King's opening gambit was his attempt to secure the magazine at Hull, which had been originally assembled for the war against the Scots. The carefully calculated move came to nothing, Sir John Hotham, the Governor, refused him entry and so Hull became the first stronghold outside London to declare openly for Parliament. By the middle of May, an armed conflict seemed inevitable. At York the King required the gentry of the county to attend him in arms on the 12th May, while in London, City regiments had been reviewed by Philip Skippon as early as the 10th May. '*Persuaded by evil counsellors*', the Commons stated, the King meant to make war on his Parliament. To prevent his doing so, Parliament reversed the situation by virtually declaring war on the King. The order was dated the 27th May 1642. During July, most of the Navy went over to the Parliament, thus ensuring that the King's vital supply line to the Continent was imperilled. Arms and ammunition, men and money, intended for the Royalists could not use any of the North Sea ports, except Tynemouth and Newcastle.

A great many held back, hoping that mediation would provide a palliative to both sides and, less politically, engaged themselves in preparing for the coming harvest. The remainder began to arm themselves and marched to whichever standard they proposed to follow. Early in July, the Parliamentarians appointed the Earl of Essex to be Captain-General of their army. Beloved of his men, 'Old Robin' was an experienced, if not particularly inspired officer. For some time Charles remained at York recruiting men, while in the Commons a Royalist advance on London was daily expected and feared. It was August before Charles marched, and even then he went only as far as the Midlands with a tiny army numbering but a few thousand. Via Coventry, which was under intermittent siege by a Parliamentarian force too undisciplined to be called an army, the King moved to Nottingham, where he made an open response to the Parliament's order of the 27th May by raising his standard on the 22nd August and proclaiming the Parliament and its servants *traitors*. This formality, carried out as it was in the centre of an area which Charles had relied upon for support, might have been expected to produce a flood of eager recruits. As it was, foul weather and insidious Parliamentarian propaganda reduced the flow of potential soldiers to a trickle and the King, while still engaged in negotiating peace terms, found himself in a weak position.

The most notable adherents to join the King at Nottingham were his two nephews, the Princes Rupert and Maurice, the third and fourth sons of his sister, Elizabeth, the exiled Queen of Bohemia. Now living in the Hague, Elizabeth was helping Queen Henrietta Maria to raise money for the purchase of cannon and arms. Rupert brought with him a train of professional soldiers which included a French mercenary, Bartholomew de la Roche, and a Walloon engineer, Bernard de Gomme. Rupert had some years experience in the European theatre of war. Although only 22, he had served in two notable campaigns in the Spanish Netherlands, and fought at Breda in 1637 and at Rheinberg in 1632. He had become a Colonel of Horse at 18 when, at the battle of Vlotho (or Lemgo) in 1638, he was captured and confined for three years in Linz Castle, a prisoner of the Emperor Ferdinand III. Of all the King's generals, Rupert's charisma was to leave the most lasting impression on friends and foe alike. One either loved or hated the Prince, but it was impossible to be indifferent to him. Charles made him General of the Horse and Rupert at once began to build up the cavalry that was to become legendary.

Royalists and Parliamentarians alike were now busy securing and fortifying strongholds throughout the land. Sporadic fighting occurred, though neither side engaged in any notable exploit; England was still largely in the hands of enthusiastic amateurs whose zeal outstripped their performance. The larger towns tended to declare for Parliament, and soon Bristol, Plymouth, Liverpool and Dover were all, willingly or unwillingly, in the hands of the Roundheads.

Some towns however had divided loyalties. When, on the 28th August, the Royalist, Sir John Byron approached Oxford, the townsfolk tried to refuse him admittance while the University welcomed his arrival with joy. The latter won the day. Leicester, hovering on the brink of a declaration, received a demand from Prince Rupert for £2000 as the price for immunity from plunder. Schooled on the Continent, Rupert regarded this as a perfectly legitimate means of raising money, a commodity of which the Royalists were always short. The frightened Mayor sent all he could muster, totalling £500, and although Charles disowned his nephew's action, there is no evidence that he ever returned the money. Leicester, not unnaturally, declared shortly afterwards for the Parliament. Rupert's reputation was not enhanced. His action earned him

Prince Rupert

the nickname of Prince Robber and added to the fables already beginning to surround his name.

In the South the King lost Portsmouth during August. Blockaded by the Navy and fired upon from Gosport and Southsea, the Royalist Governor, Colonel George Goring, felt he could not continue to hold out when further resistance could lead to mutiny in the town. Charles rightly regarded the loss of Portsmouth as a major disaster, for even without a Navy, and with France lukewarm to his cause, it would still have been possible to bring supplies into Portsmouth, for the Parliament had insufficient warships to establish a complete blockade.

At the beginning of September, Essex left London and joined his raw army at Northampton. Meanwhile, Sir John Byron had taken the plate of the Oxford colleges to Worcester which, though its defences were in a poor state of repair, was considered to be tenable as a garrison. Rupert, with eight troops of horse and 10 companies of dragoons, amounting to approximately 1,000 men, was sent to support Byron. When on the 23rd September he arrived at Worcester, the prince decided that the city was untenable and accordingly ordered a withdrawal, which he himself covered from a position at Powick Bridge. Parliamentarian horse and dragoons from Essex' army, marching ahead of the main force to join Gloucestershire troops on their way to Worcester, were not far from Powick when Rupert arrived. Having posted his men, the Prince allowed them to snatch some rest. The cavalry were in a depression north of the River Teme, and the dismounted dragoons were lining the hedges of the lane running down to the River.

Before dawn, the Roundhead commander, Colonel John Brown arrived with his force, also about 1,000 strong, at Powick Ham, south of the river. He had been there all day, awaiting some news of the advance of Essex' force, but had failed to reconnoitre forward of his position and therefore had no idea of

54

the Royalists' presence. It was 4 p.m. before a message arrived to tell him of the approach of Essex' army and it was then decided to march at once. A 'forlorn hope' crossed the bridge and advanced up the lane north of the river, to be fired upon by the Royalist dragoons, who thus alerted their horse to the approach of the enemy. Colonel Edwin Sandys, Brown's impetuous second-in-command, pushed up the lane at some speed and deployed in the field beyond. Rupert was faster however, and with no time to don their armour the Royalist horse charged the disorganised Roundheads and wrought considerable havoc on them. Sandys fell and his men broke. Only Nathaniel Fiennes' troop held firm, receiving the charge of Sir Lewis Dyve, but it was split up in the melée and driven back together with four fleeing troops. The Royalists charged home, beating the Roundheads back to the bridge where Brown's dragoons checked their victorious progress. The survivors of the fight fled back to Essex' army, fearing the Royalist pursuit more than their commander's scorn. Parliamentarian losses were, not surprisingly, heavier than those suffered by the Royalists. The Parliamentarians found it sinister that Rupert, in the forefront of the fighting and without his armour, did not receive a scratch – an immunity he was to enjoy almost until the end of the war.

The significance of Powick Bridge lay neither in the numbers wounded, nor in any strategic gain. It was purely psychological for it set the tone for much of the cavalry fighting in the first year of the war. It was a long time before the Roundheads trained troopers to stand against Rupert's terrible horsemen.

*   *   *

The King at last began his march on London on the 12th October. As his army wended its way slowly south, hampered by bad roads and cumbrous transport, on the 19th October Essex moved south-east from Worcester towards Warwick, intending to intercept the Royalist line of march. On the 22nd October, the Parliamentarian leader had reached Kineton, moving slowly because of the lack of draught horses. Both armies were so immersed in their own manifold problems that they failed to reconnoitre sufficiently, with the result that they collided haphazardly at Edgehill.

When Essex arrived at Kineton after dark on the Saturday evening, the Royalists were already quartered in an area stretching from Edgecote to Cropredy, west of Banbury. A reconnaissance force, under Lord Digby, had tried but failed to find any trace of the Roundheads. Rupert's quartermasters, still hunting for billets in Wormleighton where the Prince himself was quartered, met their Roundhead counterparts on the same errand. By sending a patrol to Kineton, Rupert discovered that Essex' men were there in force and informed the King that night. Charles took the advice offered by his nephew and ordered his army to rendezvous on the summit of Edgehill. Essex, unaware of the move, did not stir that night but, informed that Banbury was the Royalist objective, resolved to march to its relief. At dawn the following morning, Rupert's cavalry was already in position on Edgehill, awaiting the arrival of the foot. The Roundheads heard of this concentration at 8 o'clock when Essex was on his way to church. They began to form up at once between Kineton and Edgehill under the eyes of the Royalist high command, who were able to observe the Parliamentarian dispositions from their lofty vantage point. The Royalists had about 3,000 horse and dragoons, 9,000 foot and 20 pieces of artillery; the Parliament had 2,000 horse and 11,000 foot, with much of their artillery still en-route.

As the Roundheads formed up, the Royalists moved their horse down the slope, which was far too steep for cavalry action,

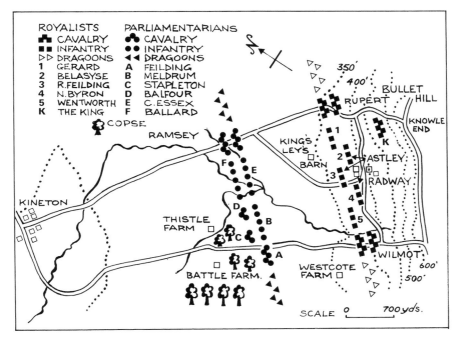

The Battle of Edgehill, 1642

the Royalist foot coming up in the centre. It was now that the lack of unified command began to tell. The Earl of Lindsey was Lord General with nominal jurisdiction over all the Royalist forces, but Prince Rupert's commission contained a clause exempting him from receiving orders from anyone except the King. The result was a divided Council of War which bred factions and disagreements. Casting his experienced eye over the dispositions, Lindsey recommended the use of the traditional Dutch formations he had learned on the continent, while Rupert insisted that the Swedish brigade system evolved by Gustavus Adolphus, would be more effective. Rupert was backed by Patrick Ruthven, Lord Forth, a veteran of the Swedish wars. When Charles decided to follow his nephew's advice,

Lindsey threw down his baton and refused to command the army any longer preferring, he said, to serve as a colonel at the head of his regiment, since the King did not think fit to repose confidence in his judgement. It was an inauspicious beginning. Charles, however, temporarily replaced him with Sir Jacob Astley, Sergeant-Major-General of the Foot, a competent veteran of the Dutch wars who was also a friend of the Queen of Bohemia and had once been Rupert's tutor.

The battle opened with an artillery duel. Despite the fact that Essex had not all his artillery with him; the Parliamentarians came off somewhat better, having the advantage of ricochet off the slope which was denied to the Royalists. Casualties were slight on both sides. While the commanders issued last minute instructions, the King on politics, Rupert on tactics, Sir Jacob Astley uttered his famous prayer: *'O Lord, Thou knowest how busy I must be this day. If I forget Thee, do not Thou forget me.'* Then, as the dragoons on both sides cleared the flanking hedges of their opponents' musketeers, the Royalist horse under Rupert on the right wing advanced down the slope towards Sir James Ramsey's forces, trotting, cantering, then galloping, holding their fire, as instructed, until they had engaged. They barely made contact with the enemy, however, before the opposing wing, having given fire out of range and seen the defection of Sir Faithful Fortescue's troops, turned rein and ran. Rupert's men, having by now built up impulse for the impact, swept on after the broken Parliamentary troops. The reserve of the Royalist right under Sir John Byron followed suit, carried away by the impetus of the first charge. On the left, Lord Wilmot broke Lord Fielding's regiment and was followed in the same fashion by *his* reserve under Lord Digby. The wholesale departure of the Royalist horse, however victorious their initial charge, left the flanks of the body of foot vulnerable, for no cavalry commander was able to rally enough men to return to

58

The Illustrious Lord, Robert Deureux Earle of Essex and Ew. Viscount
Hereford Baron of Ferrers of Chartley. Lo:Bourchier & Louain, &c.

VIRTVTIS COMES.   INVIDIA

BASIS CONSTATIA
VIRTVTVM

If Bounty. Courage. Curtesie Desert
Of noblest choice. could haue beē shew by Art
This one PIECE had exprest Them ALL in THIS
Liues what perfection can or BEE or Is.
Essex: heyre to his FATHER: by his blood.
His birth. his honours GREAT his virtues GOOD.
What Time can add to Meritt for approu'd.
In ESSEX must last happy. that's BE
LOV'D.

Earl of Essex

the field in support of the infantry. As a result, the Royalist foot fared badly. Astley had advanced his men to engage the enemy and although some of the Roundheads broke, discouraged and dismayed by the rout of their cavalry on both wings, the contest was fairly even until two Roundhead regiments of horse, those of Sir William Balfour and Sir Philip Stapleton who had escaped Wilmot's charge, fell on the left flank of the Royalist foot. Lindsey, fighting at the head of his regiment, was mortally wounded and captured. Sir Edmund Verney, the King's standard bearer, was killed and his standard taken. The Royalist foot was being slowly but steadily pushed back when at last their cavalry began to drift back. As night fell, the two sides disengaged and drew back through sheer exhaustion. The antagonists remained on the field that night. Although some 1,500 men died in the battle, it produced no decisive result. The Parliamentarians, though claiming a victory, withdrew towards Warwick the next day, leaving the Royalists in possession of the field. Although no great tactical advantage was gained by either side, the strategic outcome was undoubtedly in the Royalists' favour; Essex had attempted but failed to block their route to London. The King now had a chance to march on London before Essex could reach the capital himself.

*   *   *

In the event, both armies took some time to organise themselves sufficiently and when the Royalists did move, they advanced not on London but on Banbury. The town fell shortly after the King's guns opened fire on its defences on the 27th October. It was suggested by Prince Rupert that a small force should make a dash to London in the hope of being able to force the dissolution of Parliament. The proposal was not accepted, however, and the Royalists marched instead to Oxford. The

60

city, which was to become the King's headquarters and capital throughout the First Civil War, was occupied on 29th October, but the majority of the Army moved on almost immediately. The King entered Reading on the 4th November, but meanwhile the previously panic-stricken citizens of London had hardened in their resolve. The Trained Bands were called out and on the 8th November, Essex entered the city at the head of his field army. The Royalists tried to take over Windsor Castle on the 7th November, hoping to cut the flow of barge traffic along the Thames into London, but the Governor, Colonel John Venn MP, remained defiant and the stronghold was not attacked. On the 11th November, the Royalists reached Colnbrook where they were met with a deputation from the House of Commons bearing peace terms. Charles received them but ordered Rupert to attack Brentford the following day.

The small town of Brentford was garrisoned by two regiments of foot, those of Lord Brooke and Denzil Holles. The Prince, aware that the Trained Bands were on the move, assumed that no truce existed despite the deputation, and attacked in the early morning of 12th November. The town was carried after fierce street fighting and the Roundheads were driven back to the Thames. Many of them drowned; a few managed to swim to safety but the Royalists took over 500 prisoners, 11 colours and 15 cannon. A further loss to the Roundheads were barges containing troops, arms and ammunition. Fired upon from the grounds of Sion House, one barge blew up, several others were sunk and the rest were captured.

Meanwhile, the London Trained Bands and Essex' troops, had drawn up on Turnham Green, facing not more than 1900 Royalists who were less well equipped than the Roundheads with London behind them. The Royalists withdrew to Hounslow, their retreat covered by Astley and Rupert. From here the King could have moved round London and joined his supporters in Kent, to try and take London from the South-East. Instead, however, Charles retired to Reading which he reached on the 19th November. Both armies now went into winter quarters, Essex around London and the King near Oxford.

As the main campaigns of 1642 ended, the Royalists began to thrust westwards, making small-scale attacks along the route from Oxford towards the West Country. On the 8th December Marlborough was taken by Lord Wilmot. In the West, a secondary episode, the Royalists after initial successes had been driven out of Somerset. The Marquis of Hertford had taken the Royalist infantry, guns and baggage across the Avon into Wales, joining the King later, in time to take part in the battle of Edgehill. Sir Ralph Hopton had moved into Cornwall with only 110 Horse and 50 dragoons where, by the end of 1642, he was engaged in raising an army with the help of the famous group of Cornish Cavaliers which included Sir Bevil Grenvile, Sir Nicholas Slanning, Colonel John Trevannion and Colonel William Godolphin. Attempts on Plymouth and Exeter both failed, but by the beginning of 1643, the Royalist army in the West was welding itself into a formidable fighting force with Hopton emerging as its undisputed leader.

5. The Campaign of 1643

"... there did hardly one week pass in the summer half year, in which there was not a battle or skirmish fought, or beating up of quarters;"...

CAPTAIN RICHARD ATKYNS
Prince Maurice's Regiment of Horse

The unity which the Royalist advance on London gave to the campaign of 1642, no longer existed when the armies took the field again in 1643. The capital, of course, remained the King's main objective, but his main or 'Oxford' army was checked by one of at least equal force, commanded by the Earl of Essex and backed by the London Trained Bands. To clear the North and the West, and follow up with a triple advance on London was perhaps the most hopeful strategy for the Cavaliers, and there is some evidence that this was appreciated at Oxford. It is at least a concept which gives some sort of military logic to the widely dispersed operations of 1643.

Perhaps because of the milder climate, the commanders in the West Country sent their armies into winter quárters at the end of November. The first major action of 1643 took place at Braddock Down (19 January) when the Royalists routed General Ruthin. The Cornish infantry advanced with such resolution that the Roundheads barely stayed long enough to receive the first charge before breaking and running back to Liskeard, where the town promptly rose against them. The pursuing Royalists entered the town and took between 1,250 and 1,500 prisoners, with baggage, ammunition and arms as well as five cannon. The victory gave the Royalists control of Cornwall and they now resolved to invade Devon. Although hindered by the refusal of the Cornish Trained Bands to cross the Tamar, they took Saltash (22nd January) capturing 140 men, 4 cannon and a ship of 16 guns. Their army was too weak to besiege Plymouth, the prime objective, but a blockade was attempted. During a skirmish at Chagford, the poet Sidney Godolphin (1610-1643) *"... as gallant a gentleman as the world had ..."* was killed at Chagford (9th February). The Roundheads now counter-attacked the Royalist blockading army (21st February) and drove it back across the Tamar. On 28th February a 40-days armistice was agreed, during which time both sides recruited and rearmed. On the 25th April, three days after the expiry of the truce, the Cavaliers heard that the Roundheads planned to make a night march and attack them the following morning. The Royalists concentrated, but over-confident, failed to keep a good look-out, and were surprised whilst marching by night across Sourton Down and their advanced guard was routed. The Roundhead commander, James Chudleigh, then sent into Okehampton for his infantry to finish the disordered Royalists off. Hopton and others made a stand by their cannon, planting stakes in a convenient ditch. The Parliamentarian foot advanced but two salvoes from the Royalist cannon broke them and a charge by the Roundhead horse was brought up short by the stakes. Despite this, Sourton Down was a victory for the Parliament, the Royalists withdrawing in disorder to Brides-towe, leaving weapons, horses and powder on the field, as well as Hopton's own portmanteau. The Roundheads now prepared to follow up their victory and the Earl of Stamford crossed the Tamar into Cornwall on the 15th May, to take up a strong

64

Ralph Hopton

position at Stratton. The Royalists deployed on the night of the 15th May, and at dawn Hopton sent in his foot in converging columns. The two forces were engaged in an even contest until about 3 p.m. when James Chudleigh launched a counter-attack. The Cornish, by now short of ammunition, were thrown into some disorder but the Royalists repulsed the attack and captured Chudleigh before continuing. The Roundheads were driven from the hill, leaving behind 300 dead and 1700 prisoners and their artillery.

The victory at Stratton opened the way for Hopton to join forces with the Marquis of Hertford and Prince Maurice in Somerset, which he did at Chard on the 4th June. Meanwhile, Sir William Waller, campaigning in the West Midlands, had abandoned Hereford which he could not afford to garrison, and was making an attempt on Worcester. The news of Stratton brought him post-haste into Somerset.

In February, Waller had been given command of the Western Association, and had set up his headquarters at Bristol in March. His operations had been largley successful, though he suffered a check at Ripple (13th April) at the hands of Prince Maurice, who was immediately required to take part in an attempt to relieve Reading, and so had to march out of the Severn Valley.

From Oxford, Prince Rupert had marched to take Cirencester (2nd February), pushing Royalist communications further towards their western forces and threatening the Severn Valley where Bristol and Gloucester were in Parliamentarian hands.

*   *   *

In the Midlands, the Parliamentarians under Lord Brooke seized Lichfield Close in March. The Earl of Northampton took a Royalist force and prepared to march on Lichfield, while a

Parliamentarian force under Gell and Sir William Bereton joined hands at Hopton Heath to oppose the cavaliers. On the 19th March, the Cavaliers routed the horse and took several guns before darkness fell and the Roundhead foot was able to retreat.

The Parliamentarians lost 500 men compared with the Royalists' 50, but the latter included the Cavalier commander, the Earl of Northampton and many senior officers. Despite their victory they did not press on to Lichfield. To rectify this situation, Rupert himself was sent north from Oxford to besiege the town. On the way, he sacked Birmingham (3rd April) and took Lichfield itself a week later, although the Close itself continued to hold out. On the 21st April, the garrison in the desecrated Cathedral surrendered after Rupert had exploded the first mine laid in England. The place was then garrisoned by

Civil War infantry in review

the Royalists adding another link to the chain of fortresses securing the tenuous communications between Oxford and the Northern forces whose Headquarters were in York. Rupert himself then returned to Oxford for, in the Thames Valley, Essex had now bestirred himself and during April laid siege to Reading, an important stronghold in the ring of towns defending Oxford. The King sent to Lichfield for Rupert, but the relief force was baffled at Caversham Bridge (25th April) and Reading fell on the 27th April. The Royalists retired to Oxford and the Roundheads advanced to Thame and began to extend their hold on the Chilterns, moving on Islip, the occupation of which would give the Parliamentarians control of the Cherwell above Oxford. About this time, a Scottish soldier of fortune, Colonel John Urry deserted to the Royalists and supplied them with details of the Roundhead dispositions. He told them of a convoy bringing £21,000 to Essex for the payment of his troops. Rupert decided to attack the Roundheads and left Oxford on the afternoon of the 17th June with three Regiments of horse, some dragoons and commanded foot, a small force of about 2,000 men in all. It was the sort of operation at which the Prince excelled. Moving fast down the London Road, the force crossed the Thames at Chislehampton, attacked Postcombe early on the 18th June and pushed on to Chinnor, unluckily missing the convoy. As Rupert fell back towards Oxford, Roundhead horse and dragoons began to harass his rear. At Chalgrove Field he turned on them and in a sharp action inflicted a defeat, chiefly important because on this field John Hampden was mortally wounded.

In the west meanwhile, Waller had been unable to prevent the junction of Hopton with Maurice and Hertford. He had advanced as far as Wells before being forced to retreat hurriedly before the determined onslaught of the Royalists. The Roundheads were beaten back through the Mendips, skirmishing all the way to Bath; there was a dashing affair at Chewton Mendip (10th June). The Royalists attempted to skirt Bath in order to occupy Landsdown to the north of the city and thus cut Waller's communications with London. They reached Batheaston by the evening of 3rd July and that night Waller anticipated their next move by occupying Landsdown himself. Pre-empted, the Royalists decided not to press the engagement any further and withdrew towards Marshfield. Waller, however, was ready to give battle from his advantageous position; Landsdown drops at its North end into a deep valley up which the Cavaliers would have to advance if they chose to attack. Waller decided to lure them into doing so and harried their retreat throughout the 4th July, until a Royalist Council of War decided to stand and give battle. On the following day Waller maintained his attacks, and finally sent a party of horse and dragoons into the valley and up Freezing Hill on the other side where the Royalist cavalry, under Prince Maurice and The Earl of Caernarvon, was drawn up. The Roundhead charge, small though it was, put most of the Royalist horse to ignominious flight, leaving only the foot which, composed chiefly of pugnacious Cornish pikemen, at once advanced on Waller's formidable position in which, in the words of Colonel Walter Slingsby *"thus fortifyed stood the foxe gazing at us..."* Musketeers on either flank cleared the hedgerows of the enemy and swung round in a wide arc while the pikemen, repulsed twice just below the summit of the hill, finally gained the ridge with their musketeers closing in to pour fire into the flanks of the enemy. During the melee, Sir Bevil Grenvile, who had led the Cornish advance, was killed at the head of his regiment. The two forces fought until nightfall, by which time Waller had been driven back about 100 yards to a stone wall behind which his forces rallied. At about 11 p.m. a great volley was fired from behind the wall by the Roundheads, after which there was silence. Suspicious, though they could still see lighted match glowing in the darkness, the Royalists sent out a scout who found the wall deserted: the Roundheads had withdrawn into Bath leaving a quantity of powder and weapons to fall into Royalist hands. Despite their victory, they too were forced to withdraw the following day, short of ammunition and supplies, a situation worsened by an explosion of some powder barrels which seriously injured the indefatigable Hopton. Waller, on the other hand, recovered quickly and left Bath on the 7th July, compelling the Royalists to retreat hurriedly as far as Devizes where their foot were immediately besieged. The horse, under Hertford and Maurice, broke out and rode to Oxford to seek reinforcement. Short of ammunition, the Royalists were reduced to using bedcord for match, and were subjected to a close siege while Waller prepared to assault them. Maurice and Hertford arrived in Oxford the day after they left Devizes to find that most of the reserves had gone to the Midlands to meet the Queen. Lord Wilmot, with three brigades, 1500 strong, made up the relief force with which Maurice rode as a volunteer, 300 of his men returning with him despite the punishing ride they had so recently undertaken. Wilmot had no foot and only two light guns which he fired in order to warn the garrison of his arrival. Waller, on the point of storming the town, turned to meet the relief force which he greatly outnumbered. The garrison, despite Hopton's urgings, suspected a Roundhead ambush and held back until the battle outside was decided. Waller drew up his army on Roundway Down, his foot in the centre, his cavalry on both wings. The Royalists drove the Roundheads '*forlone hope*' back on the main body before the main forces engaged. Waller's right wing, composed of Sir Arthur Hesilrige's cuirassiers despite their heavy armour, was routed by Wilmot's brigades, and when Waller's own brigade gave way before Sir John Byron's advance, the whole of the Roundhead horse fled in terrible

70

disorder. The Royalist horse now advanced on the foot and when their own infantry was seen approaching, the Roundhead defeat became total: Waller's army was virtually destroyed and the victory opened the way for the capture of Bristol.

In the meantime, the King and Queen were reunited at Edgehill on the 12th July, the Queen bringing with her an army and wagon-loads of much needed supplies. In the Royalist camp confidence was now at its height. Rupert, who had shadowed Essex for nearly a month in order to protect his aunt's march south, left Oxford for Bristol almost immediately. On the 23rd July, the Oxford forces joined with those of Maurice and Hertford at Westbury and the armies took up their positions around the second city of the kingdom, Rupert to the North, Maurice and Hertford to the South. Although Bristol's fortifications looked formidable, the line was too long for its garrison, for Waller had lost many of the garrison at Roundway Down. There was a small but determined Royalist faction in the city who had already almost succeeded in opening the gates to Rupert earlier in the year, and the Governor, Colonel Nathaniel Fiennes, besides being unpopular was no great soldier. On the 24th July, Rupert summoned the city to surrender. Fiennes rejected the terms and an artillery bombardment began which lasted until the assault was made on the 26th July. There had been disagreement as to how the city should be carried; those on the South favoured a close investment and mining, while to the North, where the ground was rocky and the defences were weaker, it was decided to storm. The latter course was chosen, but on the morning of the assault, the Cornish to the south of the Avon anticipated the signal and advanced before dawn, forcing the troops on the north to do likewise. It was to the North that the first breach was made, despite a fierce defence by the garrison, supplemented by Puritan citizens. A party of Royalist horse got inside the line

71

through a breach made by Colonel Henry Washington's dragoons, only to be met by an inner line behind which the garrison and its reinforcements were fighting with redoubled energy. Rupert, who was present in the front line throughout the assault, requested 1,000 Cornish infantry from his brother, Maurice. They could not be supplied; the Cornish infantry had suffered heavily in a courageous but futile attempt to scale the walls to the south of the city. Maurice himself came with 500 men in the late afternoon, but by the time he arrived Fiennes had asked for terms.

The capture of Bristol added its brightest star to the galaxy of Royalist successes, while dimming still further the waning fortunes of Parliament.

*   *   *

In London, chaos threatened to choke the Roundhead war effort. Waller, complaining that his defeat at Roundway Down had been due to Essex' lack of support, was engaged in an acrimonious quarrel with the Earl while the rest of London took sides and further fragmented a disunified command. Essex was mortified still more deeply by the appointment of Waller to an independent command while his own men deserted through sickness, lack of pay and low morale. While the Parliament

Two-handed pole-axe engraved with the
Arms of the Commonwealth

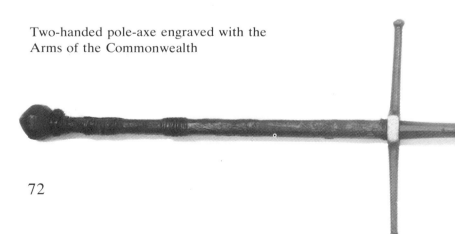

wavered, the Royalists once again split their forces, the Western army reaping a rich harvest in Dorset where Caernarvon
took Dorchester, Weymouth, Portland and Devon, while only
Exeter and Plymouth still held out against Maurice. In Dorset
only Lyme Regis was still unconquered. The Oxford army had
two alternatives, either to march on London which was so torn
by strife, that in the opinion of half the Council of War it was
ripe for the picking, or to lay siege to Gloucester. As the last
major Roundhead stronghold on the Severn, Gloucester barred
completely free access to Wales, a rich source of recruits for the
Royalists, to whose cause the Welsh largely adhered. It was
believed that the Governor, Colonel Edward Massey, might be
induced to desert the Parliamentarian cause, and the latter
course was adopted. The King led his army to summon the city.
Massey, however, refused to surrender and an investment was
begun on the 10th August, much to Rupert's disgust, for he
advocated storming the place much as he had stormed Bristol.
Charles rejected this course of action as too costly and certainly
Bristol had cost the Royalists a heavy toll, including many
officers of rank. The siege of Gloucester was not a success, for
although it was pressed with vigour, the citizens of Gloucester
proved staunchly resolute. Their resolve hardened attitudes in
London, and Essex, reinforced by five Regiments of Trained
Bands, was sent to Massey's relief Shadowed by Wilmot and
Rupert, Essex made his way via Hounslow, Beaconsfield,
Aylesbury and Stow-in-the-Wold, to Gloucester. Although
Massey had almost run out of powder, Charles raised the siege
on the 5th September. Gloucester was relieved, but Essex's

problems were far from over. Charles' intention was to cut off his retreat and prevent him from returning to London. Essex tried to draw the Royalists north, pretending that he intended to cross the Severn at Tewkesbury and march into Wales. The King ignored this move however, and himself advanced to Pershore from where he could cover Essex' return route through Evesham and Warwick. Essex, now moved south, intending to march by a road which Charles was not covering. As he moved east towards London, the King took a parallel road about ten miles to the North and the march became a race, Essex trying to reach the capital before Charles could cut him off and force him to fight. Both sides well knew that a Royalist victory could destroy the main Parliamentarian army and virtually decide the outcome of the War. The Roundheads developed a lead over the Royalists as they neared Newbury but Rupert fell on their rear at Aldbourne Chase, and seriously delayed them. Rupert seized Newbury and the Royalists were therefore able to take quantities of stores collected in the town to provision the Roundheads. Charles now stood directly in Essex path, the latter having withdrawn his army to Enborne, west of Newbury. Both commanders had something like 14,000 men at their disposal; the Roundheads with slightly more infantry than the Royalists, their true strength lying in the presence of the staunch London Trained Bands. The Royalists were also short of ammunition and there was some dispute as to whether the battle should be joined immediately. Objections were overruled and parties were sent out to secure the plateau over which the battle was to be fought. By failing to secure the hills past which the Roundheads would have to march to Reading, the Royalists allowed Essex to occupy several vital high points overlooking the field. Rupert secured the common and the guns were brought up. The land was very enclosed and unsuitable for sweeping cavalry actions of the sort that the Royalists were

74

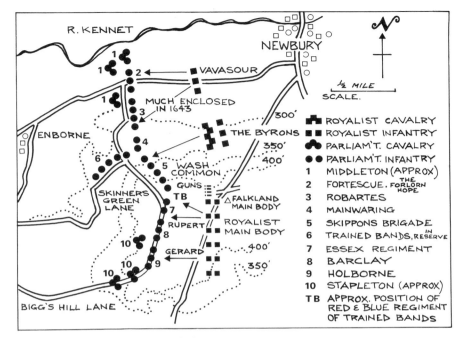

First Battle of Newbury, 1643

The map contains the following labels and legend:

R. KENNET

NEWBURY

VAVASOUR

MUCH ENCLOSED IN 1643

ENBORNE

THE BYRONS

300'
350'
400'

WASH COMMON

GUNS

SKINNERS GREEN LANE

TB

FALKLAND MAIN BODY

RUPERT

ROYALIST MAIN BODY

GERARD

400'
350'

BIGG'S HILL LANE

½ MILE SCALE.

■ ROYALIST CAVALRY
■■ ROYALIST INFANTRY
● PARLIAM'T. CAVALRY
●● PARLIAM'T. INFANTRY
1 MIDDLETON (APPROX)
2 FORTESCUE. THE FORLORN HOPE
3 ROBARTES
4 MAINWARING
5 SKIPPONS BRIGADE
6 TRAINED BANDS, IN RESERVE
7 ESSEX REGIMENT
8 BARCLAY
9 HOLBORNE
10 STAPLETON (APPROX)
TB APPROX. POSITION OF RED & BLUE REGIMENT OF TRAINED BANDS

accustomed to undertake. The Royalist infantry soon began to run short of ammunition and failed to put up an effective defence. Rupert sent his men round to attack the Roundhead infantry from the flank and rear and the Trained Bands faltered until Essex came up to reinforce them with more pikemen. The battle was initially confused and fairly even but the Royalists' shortage of powder gradually began to tell on them and they had to fall back on Newbury. The fighting went on until after dark when the Royalists withdraw into the town. The King had suffered high casualties at the battle, Rupert's attacking cavalry being especially vulnerable as they had been so circumscribed by the enclosures. Among the dead were Lord Falkland, Secretary of State, and the Earl of Caernarvon, Lord Sunderland. A Council of War was called by the Royalists. Rupert and Sir

John Byron advocated taking up the fight again the following day but the King, wavering, decided to draw back when Percy, Master of the Ordnance, informed him that ammunition was dangerously low, and in the event the Royalists withdrew northwards towards Oxford. Rupert harried the Roundheads that night before rejoining the King's army, and Essex, unaware that the Royalists had withdrawn, fired a volley into their deserted lines before advancing. Although neither side had gained a decisive victory, the Roundheads were left with the advantage just as the Royalists had been after Edgehill.

Elsewhere, the Royalists had met with mixed success. Maurice had taken Exeter just as the King raised the siege of Gloucester, and Waller and Hopton were active in Hampshire and Sussex. Hopton took Arundel Castle in December, although Waller recaptured it at the beginning of January 1644.

Disassociated with these campaigns had been actions in the North and East. In the North, the King's forces were commanded by William Cavendish, the Earl of Newcastle, who had no military experience whatsoever. His main object was to join forces with Royalists in the Eastern Counties and march to the King but he was pitted against two clever Roundhead generals, Sir Thomas Fairfax and Oliver Cromwell. Newcastle gained successes at Seacroft Moor on the 30th March and at Adwalton on the 30th June but detachments of his army were beaten at Grantham, Gainsborough and Winceby. Although Newcastle was capable of leading his force to victory, he was too indolent a commander, besides lacking any military or tactical experience. At the end of 1643, the King was no nearer victory than he had been twelve months earlier. The Royalists had gained several important successes but while their morale had been raised, the resolve of the Parliament had hardened. The fruits of this labour were soon to be felt.

6. The Campaign of 1644

The new year, 1644, saw actions by five separate Royalist armies and, ranged against them, the several armies of the Parliament, allied to that of the Scots. At the end of 1643 Parliament had negotiated an alliance with the Scots who had for a long time refused to involve themselves with the internecine quarrels which divided England; they had their own separate difference with the King and wanted to fight it out separately. When, however, James Graham, Earl of Montrose, joined the King in 1643, taking with him details of the Scottish plans, the leaders of the Covenant saw no alternative but to respond to overtures made by the Parliament. Early in 1644, a Scottish army, under the Earl of Leven, crossed the Tweed into England, while, north of the border, both Royalists and Covenanters armed and recruited.

In the South, Hopton's army had wintered in Hampshire and Sussex, beaten out of first Arundel and then Alton by Waller. They moved west to Winchester and from there, reinforced by Irish elements who had come up under Lord Forth, began to pressure the Parliamentarians until they were forced to give battle. On the 27th March, the Royalists met the Parliamentarians drawn up between East and West Meon and, deploying on top of a hill, tried to tempt Waller out of his advantageous position. Waller refused to be drawn, and instead ordered his army to march on to Alresford. Hopton, to whom command of the army had been delegated, as Forth had an attack of gout, realised Waller's intention and ordered the Royalists to march for the same destination. The final stages of the march were literally a race which the Royalists narrowly won, forcing the Roundheads to camp south of the town that night. The Royalists drew out of Alresford the following day and deployed with their backs to the town, north-east of the village of Cheriton, facing Waller's force. Skirmishing by the picquets went on during the day, but the two armies did not engage and spent the night of the 28th March in the field. On the morning of the 29th March, Hopton and Waller both drew up in battle order though Hopton suspected early in the day that his opponent meant to retire. Waller had a force in Cheriton Wood which threatened the Royalist's left. A party of Royalist musketeers drove the Roundheads out of this position giving Hopton undisputed possession of the ridge along which his forces were placed. Although Forth and Hopton had agreed to remain on the defensive, the foot on the right wing engaged the Roundheads without orders – probably because its commander, Colonel Henry Bard, saw Waller's men advancing into the dip between the two armies and saw an opportunity to attack them. He, in turn, was attacked by Hesilrige whose cuirassiers were on the Roundhead's left and they fell on the unsupported Royalist foot, annihilating the first regiment. Following this, Balfour attacked Hopton's foot on the left wing. This held its ground, although with difficulty and when a party of horse, sent to attack Hesilrige's men, were worsted in a sharp fight, the Royal-

Oliver Cromwell

ists began to withdraw. They moved back to Tichborne Down, south of Alresford, but they were hard pressed and Hopton and Forth, once again consulting, decided to retire. This they did, via Basing House, which they reached in the early hours of the 30th March, and then to Reading. Waller did not deign to pursue his beaten opponents, but went on to Winchester. The town fell on the 30th March, though the castle continued to defy him. Following the Royalist defeat at Cheriton, the King effectively disbanded Hopton's army, amalgamating it with his own and ordering Forth and Hopton to join him at Oxford. At the same time, the Royalist garrison at Reading was withdrawn. The victory to the Roundheads raised morale among Parliamentarians although the strategic implications were not significant.

*   *   *

Two sources of recruits gained importance at the beginning of the year. These were Wales and Ireland. Irish volunteers were brought into England at Chester (Liverpool was held by the Roundheads) from whence they were distributed to the areas where strength was needed. The majority of these men, however, began their military careers at Shrewsbury where Rupert had made his headquarters in January. From this strategic point, the Prince was able to arrange for the reception of Irish soldiers and to recruit in Wales which was easily accessible. Part of the force thus raised saw its first action when Newark, an important Royalist garrison, was tightly invested by a Roundhead force under Sir John Meldrum. On the visit to Chester, Rupert received orders to go to the relief of the town, but he was so short of troops that he had to return to Shrewsbury for reinforcements. The besieging army knew this, and calculated that there would be some delay while Rupert collected his forces. They were wrong. Although Meldrum contrived to interpose his cavalry between Rupert and his objective, the manoeuvre failed and his rapid advance forbade a repetition of the attempt. Meldrum decided to concentrate his foot in the vicinity of the Spittal, an edifice just outside the city walls where he had made his headquarters. At the same time, he sent his horse out to gather provisions. The Roundhead line of retreat, over a bridge near Muskham Fort was secured by musketeers and Meldrum felt relatively safe. Rupert suspected that his quarry was about to withdraw and quickened his march to such an extent that he arrived at Newark with a small party of horse long before the main body of his army. Meldrum's cavalry withdrew before his advance and Rupert occupied Beacon Hill from where he could view the Roundhead dispositions. Still fearing that Meldrum was going to withdraw, Rupert decided to attack with the forces he had, hoping to hold the Roundheads until the rest of his army came up. His charge was successful, despite the disparity in numbers. The fighting was fierce, especially on the right wing and Rupert himself was set upon by a Roundhead trooper whose hand was cut off by Sir William Neale who was attending the Prince. By the time the Royalist infantry came up, the main action was over and the Roundheads had been beaten back to the Spittal and the island behind. Tillier's force tried to prevent Meldrum's horse from retreating across the bridge of boats, but the Roundheads beat him off. The Royalists now decided to starve the garrison out of the Spittall, knowing that Meldrum only had enough food for two days. The Roundheads were surrounded by Rupert, Tillier and the Newark garrison and when the Governor of Newark, Sir Richard Byron, sent out a party to capture Muskham Bridge, which had been abandoned by the Roundhead musketeers, Meldrum asked for terms. The terms Rupert granted were generous, but the Royalists won useful muskets, cannon and mortars. The victory had been won at a cost of less than 100 to the Royalists while the Roundheads had lost 200 men. They marched out towards Hull on the 22nd March.

The relief of the siege of Nantwich, a town held for Parliament, had been undertaken in January that year by Sir Thomas Fairfax. The besieging force under Lord Byron had shut the forces of Sir William Bereton in the last major garrison to hold out against the King. Byron's force, split by a swollen river and outnumbered, was beaten off. It was as a direct result of this action that Rupert had been appointed to recoup the North for the King.

Still further North, Newcastle was trying to contain the inexorable advance of a Scottish army and in this he largely succeeded during the early part of the year. Visited by the Marquis of Montrose, he had given him as much help as he could in raising a Scots Royalist Army, although Newcastle himself was badly outnumbered. With poor arms and few men – and those only having been obtained after a long wrangle with the King and his supporters – Montrose was to achieve brilliant successes in Scotland.

Following Rupert's success at Newark, the Council of War, along with the rest of the King's supporters at Oxford, became more optimistic for the Midlands was now largely in the hands of the King. With Rupert continuing to fight in the north, a determined effort to defeat Waller in the south might bring a swift end to the war. The King now had three armies in the field as opposed to Parliament's five; the Oxford Army, with which Hopton and Forth's men had become allied; the Western Army, a small force under Prince Maurice, which was besieging Lyme Regis; and the Northern Army to which Rupert's force was to march since Newcastle was now immobile in York and besieged by Fairfax and the Scots. By May, the Committee of Both Kingdoms in London had decided to make an attack on Oxford which was strongly protected by a ring of garrisons. The

82

Cavalry meet infantry

danger was so great that the King sent his wife, who was pregnant, into the West Country and summoned Rupert back to Oxford. The Prince's prime intention was to relieve Newcastle at York, but he stayed at Oxford for a week during which he gave his view of the situation and how it should be dealt with. The gist of his scheme was to keep a strong ring of vital garrisons around Oxford, too strong for the Parliament to take them all, thus leaving the bulk of the King's army free to move down to the West Country to help Maurice. If Rupert was able to subdue the North, the Royalists would, by the end of the summer, be in control of most of England. Unfortunately, as soon as Rupert left Oxford, the King missed his dynamic presence and began, as was his custom, to vacillate between the opinions held by civilians in the Council – generally unfavourable to the Prince – and those of the soldiers. Digby and Forth were probably responsible for the abandonment of Reading and Abingdon, the latter only 6 miles from Oxford. Essex and Waller now began to converge on Oxford, Essex setting up his headquarters at Islip at the end of May, and Waller arriving at Newbridge, between Abingdon and Oxford, on the 1st June. The King, leaving most of his foot and heavy ordnance in his headquarters, left the city on the 3rd June and arrived at Worcester on the 4th June, evading the pursuit of Essex and Waller. The two Roundhead commanders, who did not get on well together, met during the march. At this point Essex resolved to relieve the siege of Lyme while leaving Waller to chase Charles. Had he not made this error, subsequent events in the Midlands might have turned out very differently. As it was, Essex relieved the siege and continued to march south-west. Waller, although he captured Sudeley Castle, did not succeed in catching the King, who contrived to elude his pursuers until he had doubled back from Worcester to Witney where he rejoined the garrison from Oxford.

When the Royalist Army approached Buckingham, the Committee of Both Kingdoms feared that he might mean to attack the Eastern Association and ordered Waller, who was at Gloucester, to intercept the King. By the 28th June, Waller was near Banbury and Charles at Brackley, moved towards him. On the same day the Royalists arrived north-east of Banbury and Roundhead forces occupied Crouch Hill, south-west of the town while the Royalists took up a position on Grimsbury Hill. The two armies spent the night in these positions and on the following day the King decided to try and draw Waller towards Daventry in order to try and bring him to battle on more favourable terrain. As the Royalists moved north, Waller moved on a parallel northward path, about a mile away, in full view of the opposing force. As the King approached the village of Cropredy, three miles north of Banbury, Waller halted near Bourton Hill where once again he had the advantage of ground. The Royalists sent a party of dragoons to secure their flank by holding the bridge over the Cherwell at Cropredy, a move accelerated by the approach of some Roundhead horse marching south to Waller. Waller decided to march round, seize the crossings over the Cherwell and cut off the Royalist retreat. Middleton, in command of half of the Roundhead party, facing the Royalists, skirmished with the rear and forced the dragoons holding Cropredy Bridge back on the main body. The Royalists were forced back to Hays Bridge where further retreat was stopped by a party of Royalist Musketeers who blocked the road with an overturned carriage. The other prong of the Roundhead attack was commanded by Waller. He made for Slat Mill, a ford across the Cherwell south of Cropredy, on the flank of the Royalists' extended column. His advance was so rapid that the Royal rearguard was threatened. Cleveland, the commander of the leading division of the rearguard, was temporarily saved by Northampton who charged the Roundheads and drove them back across the ford. Without awaiting orders, Cleveland then charged Middleton's men, routing his foot and some of his horse. Realising the danger, Charles sent a party of horse back to attack Middleton's horse. This force, under Lord Bernard Stuart, fell on the Roundheads who were threatening Cleveland's flank, pushing them back on to the rest of the disordered force which was then charged by Cleveland himself, Wilmot attacking on his right. After a short, sharp fight, the Roundhead horse was driven back across Cropredy Bridge into the village and their artillery, stranded on the east of the river, was captured by the Royalists. The Roundheads had been repulsed, but they still held Cropredy Bridge and the Slat Mill ford and so the Royalist main body turned south and took up a position facing Waller's force at Cropredy. The two forces engaged again at the bridge and the ford. At the former, the Royalists were not able to beat back the Roundheads, but at the latter the Royalists took the ford and put some men across onto the west bank. Only small parties were involved in these actions and it was not until the evening that the Royalists drew up at Slat Mill and turned their attention to the Roundhead horse on

Civil War cannon

Bourton Hill. This was finally repulsed in disorder. Waller claimed that although defeated, he had achieved his object in that the King had been prevented from joining Rupert in the north. The King's victory was greater; Waller's army disintegrated due to the drop in morale and the commander himself bewailed the disunity of command which had precipitated the disaster. He returned to London advocating an army raised and controlled by the Parliament. He was soon to get one. Both armies remained on the field following the battle, but when Charles heard of the approach of Major-General Browne with a Roundhead force, he moved to interpose himself between Waller and Browne, fearing they would attempt a junction. The threat came to nothing and the Royalists turned their attention to the west where Essex was looming large in the fortunes of the Queen now residing at Exeter, where she had given birth to a daughter, her eighth child, on the 16th June. The Royal Army marched west on 12th July. Rumours of a battle reported to

have taken place outside York were confirmed that night when Rupert's despatch reached the King.

*   *   *

In the north, Rupert's chief objective was the relief of the siege of York, now hard pressed by Fairfax's Northern Army, Manchester's Eastern Association and Leven's Scottish Army. He had first to secure Cheshire and Lancashire, chiefly in order to ensure the safe passage of Irish recruits and to safeguard his own passage northwards. He left Shrewsbury on the 16th May. Moving in to Cheshire, Rupert began recruiting, and reducing the Parliamentarian garrisons in his path. On the 25th May be arrived at Stockport, which he took with little difficulty in an action which forced Colonel Alexander Rigby to raise the siege of Lathom House. Rigby retired to Bolton, where Rupert arrived on the 28th May. The fall of the town, which was strongly Puritan, was accompanied by rampaging Royalist soldiers and resulted in the loss of 1,600 Roundhead lives, with considerable plundering. These three successes encouraged

Lancashire Royalists who flocked to Rupert's banner. After he had been reinforced by Goring and Sir Charles Lucas from Yorkshire, Rupert marched on to Liverpool. The defence was stout, and the Royalists sat down before the city on the 7th June but most of the garrison and its stores were evacuated by sea before the town fell on the 11th June. At this point, Rupert was delayed, partly due to the lack of ammunition expected from the south, and partly due to the Prince's own uncertainty, stemming from the King's plight in the south. Since leaving Oxford, most of the Prince's plans had been changed and when the King wrote to him from Worcester he intimated that if the situation did not improve, Rupert might well be summoned to his Uncle's side. The Prince's successes in the north were alarming the King's Councillors who were growing afraid of Rupert's military power. Rupert knew these things and was unwilling to commit the northern forces to a campaign when he might soon have to abandon the project to move south. So for this reason he delayed. During this time the King wrote again on the 14th June, assuring his nephew, in an ambiguous letter, that although he was in dire straits he might be able to hold out until Rupert moved to him, if the Prince first 'beat' the rebels in front of York. It is, even now, not clear what Charles meant by that; his nephew, characteristically, took a positive line and construed that the King wished him to disperse the armies which lay around York. Collecting his army at Preston, Rupert marched across the country, until on the 26th June he reached Skipton Castle. Here Goring rejoined him; he had gone into Cumberland to get reinforcements and arrived at Skipton with horse and foot to add to Rupert's force. From Skipton, where the Royalists halted for three days, the army moved to Knaresborough where the relieving force made contact with the besieged garrison in York by lighting a beacon in the church tower. Within the city, the Royalists had already withstood one

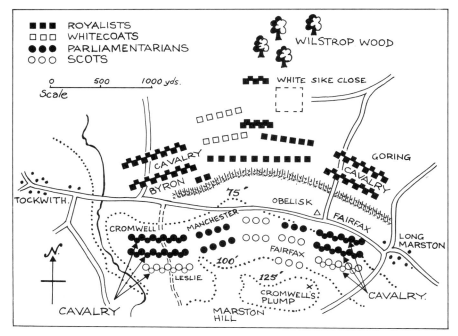

Battle of Marston Moor, 1644

major assault, repulsed when one of three Roundhead mines was exploded prematurely. The Roundheads, under General Laurence Crawford, assaulted the city walls at this point, but as he omitted to tell Leven or Fairfax of his attack, he went in unsupported and was beaten off with the loss of 200 men.

Reports of Rupert's advance were corroborated on the 1st July by the appearance of a large body of Royalist horse which drew up between the villages of Tockwith and Long Marston, west of York. The Roundheads concentrated opposite them, withdrawing from their siege and leaving every road except the western approach unguarded, with the exclusion of a bridge of boats which lay across the Ouse at Poppleton, north of the city. This was guarded by a detachment of dragoons from the Earl of Manchester's Army. The Allied forces, thinking that they faced the vanguard of Rupert's army, formed up in battle order and awaited the arrival of a more substantial body of Royalists. This did not materialise. Rupert had left Byron with a cavalry screen while he himself swung north with the bulk of this army, via Boroughbridge and Thornton Bridge, fording the rivers Ure, Swale and Ouse. The Prince made a 22-mile detour which took him in a wide sweep, enabling him to descend on the besieged city from the north. The only opposition they encountered was at Poppleton where Manchester's dragoons were overpowered. By evening, most of the Cavaliers were encamped in the Forest of Galtres, in sight of the city walls and unequivocally placed between the allies and the object of their siege. Rupert himself did not enter the town, but sent Goring in to Newcastle and Eythin while he himself reconnoitred the allied position, with a view to attacking as soon as he could. Goring bore a message to Newcastle, who was technically his commanding officer, requesting his presence on the field with his forces at dawn on the 2nd July. Newcastle, labouring with the problems of mutinous troops who were plundering the vacated siege works of the allied forces, was none too pleased by this peremptory order. Firstly, he felt (possibly correctly) that Rupert was attempting to assert his authority by forcing his hand and presenting the Marquis with a *fait accompli*. Secondly, he was genuinely at a loss to know what to do with his unruly troops who had run wild since the relief of the city. At all events, the Marquis, arriving with only a few of his troops several hours after dawn, informed the Prince that he did not consider the joining of battle to be advisable. The disparity in numbers was noticeable; the Royalists had possibly 18,000 men to the Allies 28,000 and Newcastle advocated a delay at least, since he was expecting 2,000 men under Colonel Sir Robert Clavering to reinforce him from the North. Only Rupert's assurance that the King had positively commanded him to fight persuaded him to agree.

90

The foot from the city, numbering about 3,000, arrived on the field of Marston Moor at 3 p.m. under James King, Lord Eythin, who was a professional soldier of extreme caution, a fact which had already been made known to Rupert at the battle of Vlotho in 1638. The incompatability of their personalities did not auger well and manifested itself almost immediately when a dispute arose over the disposition of the field. Shown to Eythin in the form of a sketch map, the Commander had commented laconically, *"By God, Sir, 'tis very fine on paper, but there's no such thing in the field!"* Rupert seems to have been determined to keep his temper, indeed he was even conciliating; he offered to draw the lines back and reform them, but Eythin ungraciously responded that it was now too late to do so.

The allies meanwhile, seeing that they had been soundly outmanoeuvered, and had lost their siege train and ammunition into the bargain, decided to withdraw south to Tadcaster, thence to Cawood – where there was another bridge of boats – from which point, Meldrum's advance could be covered and, hopefully, Rupert's probable march south to the King could be blocked. (News of Cropredy Bridge did not reach either side until after the 2nd July). By the time the Royalists' intention was made plain, only the rear guard under Sir Thomas Fairfax remained on the field and it was necessary to recall the rest of the army, leading elements of which had already reached Tadcaster, eight miles south. Rupert had wished to attack the retreating allies but was held back by the absence of Newcastle. When the Marquis finally arrived, he was still eager to fight, but by then, the allied strength was too great and the Prince was dissuaded. The allied forces, under the joint command of Sir Thomas Fairfax, the Earl of Leven and the Earl of Manchester, were deployed with Cromwell commanding the horse – his 'Ironsides' – on the left, interspersed with musketeers; the foot front line under Laurence Crawford and General Baillie in the centre, and the horse under Fairfax on the right. The Royalists were in a defensive position. The right wing of horse under Byron being placed behind a ditch and interspersed with musketeers – unusually for Rupert whose tactics were generally of a more aggressive nature, his horse being deployed in the Swedish rather than the Dutch formation. The foot in the centre were under Tillier and the horse on the left under Goring. Rupert himself took up a position behind the centre adjacent to White Syke Close with two regiments of horse and his lifeguard.

By the time both armies were drawn up it was evening and a thunderstorm was brewing. The Royalists settled down for the night in their positions. Cromwell chose this moment to advance on Byron's wing, who opposed him. The forlorn hope, under Napier, fell back and Byron, despite Rupert's express orders to the contrary, took the front line of horse across the ditch. The move had a two-fold effect: it negated any possible use to which the musketeers might have been put and, as the Royalists did not advance beyond this line and precipitate the engagement – which might have served them better – it left the horse in an unmanoeuvrable position, circumscribed by the ditch at their backs. The clash brought the Royalists off worst, Rupert himself rode to this wing as Byron's line broke and took in his reserve. There was a fierce fight which ended with the rout of the Royalist horse and almost concluded in the capture of the Prince himself. He escaped, however, by jumping a wall into a beanfield, then galloping down a lane to the back of the Royalist lines where he began to gather the broken horse. On the left, Goring had fared better, driving the Roundheads from the field. Another smaller charge by Newcastle in the centre, also went well for the Royalists, but Cromwell's victorious horse, better disciplined than their Royalist counterparts, was ready to return to the fray, and it methodically dispersed Goring's inferior force before turning its attention to the exposed flanks of the Royalist foot. This body, though badly outnumbered, fought very valiantly and was finally beaten into White Syke Close where the remaining regiments were more or less annihilated. The battle on Marston Moor was over by 9 p.m. and was a resounding Roundhead victory. Henceforth, the Royalists had an ever declining grasp on the North; a brilliant strategic coup had been pressed too far and turned into disaster.

The King was curiously sanguine about this. Rupert, with customary energy, tried to recoup his losses, while Newcastle and Eythin went abroad. While the Prince worked his way back through Yorkshire, Lancashire, Cheshire, Wales and eventually down to Bristol, his uncle continued his more successful campaign in the South.

*   *   *

Having relieved the siege of Lyme Regis, the Earl of Essex continued westwards to occupy Taunton on the 10th July. Plymouth was relieved on the 23rd July and from there the Earl marched into Cornwall, intending to overrun it for the Parliament. His interlude of success was short-lived. In order to remain in contact with the fleet, which was commanded by the Earl of Warwick, Essex advanced to Lostwithiel through hostile Cornish countryside. It was not long before the King, who was only marginally more popular with the Cornish, began inexorably to close in on his opponent. With 16,000 men – the sum total of the armies of Charles, Hopton, Maurice and Richard Grenvile – Charles summoned Essex with his 10,000 to surrender. Essex, hoping for the timely arrival of Waller to the rear of the Royalists refused. As the Roundheads strengthened Lostwithiel and a strip of land from there to the village of Fowey, the Royalists systematically occupied the ring of hills around the area, which gave them an unhindered view of the Roundhead position. When it became clear that not only was Waller a long way off, but also Warwick was unable to bring the fleet up due to contrary winds, Essex allowed Sir William Balfour to attempt to break out of the encirclement. This he achieved, with 2,000 horse, on the 31st August, but not before the two sides had engaged in battle. On the 21st August the King had launched his first major attack on the Parliamentarian position. All along

Charles II, when Prince of Wales – painted by William Dobson (1644)

a four mile front the Royalists moved forward, Grenvile, to the north (the right) took the Castle which overlooked Lostwithiel and outflanked the Roundhead positions on Druid's and Beacon Hills, causing the forces occupying them to retire. Little opposition was encountered until late in the day, but by then, the Royalists were securing their position on Beacon Hill and there was little they could do. Forces were sent to Par, west of Fowey, under Goring and Bassett, to prevent the landing of supplies and foraging by the Roundheads. As Charles, suspecting a Parliamentarian withdrawal to Fowey, had swung part of his force south to counteract the move, the town of Lostwithiel was now almost entirely surrounded. It was at this point that Balfour escaped, early on the 31st August. The Royalists were chagrined that he had been allowed to get away, but that day they advanced on Lostwithiel itself which they entered without encountering much opposition. By this time, the Roundheads were in full retreat southwards. The King pursued and relentlessly harried their rearguard until by nightfall it had reached Castle Dore, an Iron Age fort. The Royalists settled down in front of the Roundhead position of which Castle Dore formed the centre. During the night the Parliamentarian foot began to abandon their position and when one entire regiment – Weare's – left their place east of Castle Dore, a gap was opened up which gave the Royalists an open road to Fowey. Essex took to a boat by which he escaped to Plymouth. The Royalists prepared to renew the attack the following day – Goring had been sent to chase the Roundhead Horse – but their opponents, of whom there were now only 6,000, asked for a parley. The Cornish were chiefly responsible for the privations that caused the death of so many.

York fell on 16th July, after which the three armies which had besieged it split up, Leven to besiege Newcastle-on-Tyne, Fairfax to reduce remaining Royalist garrisons in Yorkshire and

Manchester to return to Lincolnshire. From there the army, hearing of the disaster which had befallen the Roundheads in Cornwall, continued south to join Waller. Essex had arrived in London to be greeted as if nothing had happened, but his shattered army was going to have to be rebuilt for Charles was moving east once more with his victorious forces, albeit very slowly. The Parliament assumed that the King would now march on London; nothing stood in the way of this course, but the King was more concerned with minor matters; he wished merely to relieve the garrisons of Banbury, Basing and Donnington before going into winter quarters. The armies of the Parliament, meanwhile, were rending themselves apart. The Army of the Eastern Association under Manchester was at Reading from where it declined to move. Manchester and Cromwell entertained an increasing dislike and distrust for each other. The reasons for this were largely political, but the latent hostility was exacerbated by Cromwell's unfortunate habit of claiming that the victory of Marston Moor belonged to himself and God alone. Waller was at Farnham, fuming quietly at the way Essex was forgiven his crass stupidity in the summer by the Committee of Both Kingdoms. The position of the armies, however, forbade any possibility of Charles' marching on London, if such had ever been his intention. There was still a threat that the King's army, weakened though it was by the detachments left to besiege Plymouth and Exeter, would be able to destroy these separate forces in detail. At the beginning of October, a conference took place at Sherborne Castle at which Rupert was present. It was decided that he would take a force into the field to try and lure one of the Roundhead armies into battle while the King dealt with the rest of the forces. Failing this, Rupert was to rejoin his uncle. While the Prince organized this offensive, the King advanced through Wiltshire and Hampshire, goading Manchester into action; he moved to join Essex's

96

Statue of Oliver Cromwell, Parliament Square

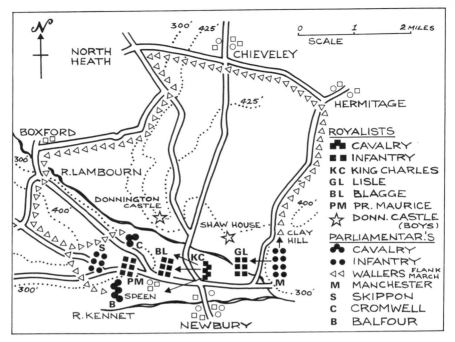

Second Battle of Newbury, 1644

foot in Hampshire while Waller moved to Andover, covering
Basing House which he was besieging. Waller was beaten out of
Andover on the day after Manchester reached Basingstoke
(18th October). The Roundhead forces concentrated around
Basingstoke to prevent the Royalists from relieving Basing
House while the King moved up via Kingsclere to Newbury
where he quartered on the night of 23rd October. The Parliamentarian armies of Essex, Manchester and Waller withdrew
from Basing to follow the King. On the 26th October, the armies
were facing each other, north of Newbury. The King held a
position which ran from Speen, through Shaw House to Donnington Castle which had been relieved by the approach of the
King's army. It was a formidable position and the Roundheads
viewed it with respect despite the fact that they had 17,500 men

98

to the King's 9,000. The Parliamentarian Council of War, a Committee, in fact, minus Essex who was in bed with a cold, decided that the only way to make an effective attack was to assault from the front and rear. The flanking march was detected, however, and Maurice moved to the west of Speen to block it. Despite this, the flanking attack was made and was successful. Speen was taken early in the battle by the Roundheads along with the redoubt Maurice had built on his position. The Royalists counterattacked, however, just before dark, and the Roundheads were driven out. At this late stage, Manchester assaulted Shaw House, the centre of the Royalist position. It was getting dark and he was repulsed although losses on both sides were small. The battle ended there, with losses of about 500 to Royalists and Parliamentarians alike. The King did not favour a renewal of the battle and left his artillery, ammunition and baggage at Donnington while the army retired to Newbury that night. The withdrawal caused the Roundhead army to claim a victory, but since their objective had been either to destroy the King's army or, failing this, to prevent it reaching Oxford, it can hardly be justly claimed as such. The King, having created his nephew commander-in-chief (although his son, the Prince of Wales had titular command) in place of the Earl of Brentford, returned to Donnington with Rupert on the 10th November. The besieged castle had already refused a summons to surrender and the appearance of a large relieving force caused a quandry in the Roundhead Council. It was finally decided not to give battle and the Parliamentarian forces withdrew enabling the Royalists to draw off unmolested. Meanwhile, Basing had also been relieved by the action at Newbury and Banbury was free. With these objectives accomplished, the King arrived in Oxford on the 23rd November. It had been a year of triumphs and disasters for both sides.

7. The Offensive of the New Model

*"Gentlemen, I beseech you let's consider what
we do. The King need not care how oft he
fights... If we fight 100 times and beat him 99
he will be King still..."*
MANCHESTER.

At the beginning of 1645, the two sides found themselves in a
state of stalemate. Neither had succeeded in destroying the
other's army and internal strife on both sides was looming large.
Changes in the high command of the King's Army had taken
place during 1644; Wilmot, who had talked too freely about
negotiating privately with Essex, had been arrested and
replaced by Goring who drank scarcely any less than his pre-
decessor, but was probably more competent and Harry Percy,
who had been a factious and inefficient General of the Ordnance, resigned, to be replaced by Lord Hopton which was an
undoubted improvement. Rupert's effective post was as
Commander-in-Chief of the Army, which, although his actual
command was only that of Lieutenant-General, inspired in his
many enemies at Court ideas of his possible treachery, which
certainly never entered his head. The suspicions, however, were
enough to prejudice his effectiveness in the field since every
request he made to the King was delivered at Court accompanied by advice and information calculated to diminish

Charles' confidence in his nephew. The situation worsened when, during an abortive attempt to re-take Abingdon in January, the Governor of Oxford, Sir Henry Gage, was killed. He was replaced by Colonel William Legge who was Rupert's best friend. Many members of the Court, notably Lord Digby, found this sinister, for it looked like a concentration of the Prince's friends in strategic positions. Since the arrival of the Elector Palatine in London in August 1644, there had been some doubts on both sides concerning the inviolability of the King's throne.

Meanwhile, things fared little better in London. After the disaster in Cornwall and the indecisive battle at Newbury in October, there was an explosion of bitter recrimination in which Manchester's tardiness and general unsuitability as a commander was lamented by Cromwell, who was in turn denounced as an extremist by Manchester. The eventual upshot of the Parliamentary disagreements was the moving of the "Self-Denying Ordinance" and the creation of the New Model Army which Sir Thomas Fairfax was to command, being the only suitable man not exempted from the post by the Self-Denying Ordinance. The House of Lords threw the bill out, understandably, since the provision in the Ordinance that members of neither House could hold military command would have forced the resignation of Essex. A modified form of it was pushed through which enabled Cromwell to be appointed Lieutenant-General.

*   *   *

The New Model Army had as its great merit the fact that it would be centrally commanded. It consisted of a force of 22,000 men made up of 11 regiments of horse, one of dragoons, and 12 battalions of foot. While this potential threat to the King was still being debated, Rupert moved into

101

Gloucestershire to do what he could to upset the wool trade there. Establishing a garrison at Chipping Campden, he proceeded to harass the towns which traded with Gloucester. This city now found itself hemmed in by Royalist Worcester, Cirencester and Chipping Campden. The Prince followed this move with an abortive attempt on Abingdon on the 11th January. It is indicative of the hardened attitudes on both sides that Major-General Browne, Governor of the town, hanged five so-called 'Irish' officers who were in fact prisoners of war and nominally immune from summary execution. Later in the year thirteen other Royalist 'Irish' were summarily hanged; Rupert replied by hanging thirteen Roundheads and, when Essex complained, replied that until the Roundheads ceased to vent their spleen by hanging prisoners of war, he would continue to carry out his policy of 'an eye for an eye'. It is true that the Parliament was vitriolic in its hatred of the Irish, but it is also interesting that Rupert, held three years earlier to be the arch-criminal in the matter of atrocities committed on soldiers and the populace, should emerge from these incidents as much the milder of the two protagonists. At all events, the hangings ceased. The north continued to crumble; Liverpool had fallen at the end of 1644 and Byron, struggling against increasingly long odds, threatened to resign unless Rupert supported him more comprehensively. In the west, Sir Richard Grenvile was besieging Plymouth but an assault was heavily repulsed due to the fact that the place had not been blockaded and the port was being supplied from the sea. Goring meanwhile, in a burst of energy, sallied forth as far as Farnham, which discomforted London somewhat until he was forced to retire.

Before the campaign of 1645 was well underway, the important Royalist centre of Shrewsbury fell in February. The Governor of the town was ill and a Parliamentary plot was hatched with the aid of sympathetic townsfolk. The town gates were

George, Lord Goring

opened to a Roundhead force on the night of the 22nd February and the Governor was among those killed in the street fighting.

Throughout the winter, the King undertook peace negotiations in which he himself placed little faith. The Commissioners at Uxbridge were, however, still at a standstill in February when the talks broke down completely.

*   *   *

Only in Scotland were circumstances more favourable to the Royalists. Montrose had originally campaigned with his pen rather than his sword, had importuned the King and Queen in person and had finally gained a commission as Lieutenant-General of Scotland. Despite this rank, he had very few men and neither Rupert nor Newcastle were in a position to provide him with troops on the two occasions he requested them in 1644. Irish troops led by Alaster M'Coll Keitach, known, for ease of pronounciation, as Alasdair Macdonald, were landed on the Scottish coast in July 1644. Working independently, Macdonald gained control of the Ardnamurchan peninsula and recruited some Highlanders, but this body proved erratic and neither Macdonald nor Montrose was able to rely on their support. This became clear when Macdonald moved inland from his base, but he contrived to rendezvous with Montrose at Blair where the Royalists were able to recruit a force. On the 1st September this army defeated the Covenanters at Tippermuir. The Royalists were pursued by the Duke of Argyll as they moved north, but Argyll was too far behind to prevent Montrose from inflicting another heavy defeat on the Covenanters at Aberdeen on the 13th September. The Royalists continued to withdraw however, still followed by the dogged Argyll. Meeting Macdonald, Montrose was prevailed upon to launch an attack on the Campbell – and Covenanting – country around

104

Loch Fyne. It was December, but the weather was mild and Montrose marched on Inverary the Campbell stronghold which was comprehensively sacked, having been taken completely by surprise. Argyll was now seriously worried; he realised that larger forces than he had at his command would be needed to eliminate the small but cunning Royalist Army. A detachment of Leven's army under William Baillie was sent to Argyll who was encamped at Inverlochy. Baillie was posted to Perth, and it was planned to crush Montrose between the two forces as he withdrew from the Campbell country. The Royalists, however, marched over the hills of Lochaber and on the 2nd February, came down to surprise and destroy Argyll's force, killing 1,500 Campbells in the process.

Montrose's success contrasted sharply with the fortunes of the Royalists further south and the King, ever one to clutch at straws, chose to regard the victories in Scotland as sufficient reason to continue his martial activities in the south. At the same time, he divided his Council sending – amongst others – Hopton, Lord Capel, Lord Culpeper and Edward Hyde to the west, where the Prince of Wales now had his own staff and Council. Much of the King's success would depend on the supply of Irish recruits; a small portion of his Council doubted the wisdom of this policy and also doubted whether the Irish were as serious in their protestations of loyalty as Charles chose to believe. It was these dissidents who were sent to Prince Charles in the west. Rupert's own opinion, that the Irish would eventually cheat the King, was more kindly received, but Charles was unswerving in his resolve. Having ascertained the King's chosen course of action, it was necessary to plan a strategy which would achieve it. Goring, chafing and dissatisfied with the ambiguous and inefficient chain of command of the west where his authority was questionable, was present at the Council called at Oxford.

Sir Thomas Fairfax

The Royalist successes in Scotland had necessitated the weakening of Leven's Scottish army in England, while, in the south, Cromwell and Fairfax were recruiting their new army which, though incomplete, was already in the field, Cromwell had moved west to harry Oxford: he had taken Bletchingdon House, for which the Governor, Colonel Francis Windebank

106

was shot, and had driven away all the pack horses in the district. Moving further west, he clashed with the Royalists at Faringdon Castle which he failed to take by storm. Fairfax on the other hand also came off the worse when he encountered Goring, with a party of horse on his way to Oxford. Fairfax was on his way to relieve Taunton which part of his force managed to do on the 11th May.

It was sound sense that the Royalists should strike where the enemy was weakest. Given that it was unlikely that Fairfax would march north to aid Leven, Rupert suggested that Chester, which was now besieged, should be relieved and the passage for the Irish levies into Lancashire and Yorkshire secured. There was also a possibility that this plan would enable the northern Royalists under Sir Marmaduke Langdale to be relieved and also that some reinforcements might be sent to Montrose. Those who disagreed with this strategy advocated bringing Fairfax to battle. It was decided that Goring should return west to hold Fairfax there while the rest of the Oxford force moved north.

As Fairfax moved on Taunton, Cromwell took a parallel course to the north of him, protecting the Fairfax force from attack by the Oxford army. This left Charles free to move north. As he did so, Fairfax was ordered to Oxford, leaving only a small force to relieve Taunton. Goring failed to intercept the Parliamentary force and when ordered back to join the main Royalist army which lay at Market Harborough he refused to do so. His position and command had at last been consolidated; he had no intention of allowing it to weaken by leaving the west. Although Fairfax sat down before Oxford on the 19th May, the King made no immediate move to go to the city's relief: the citizens had been ordered to lay in six months' provisions the previous winter and there was no danger that Fairfax would storm the city. A portion of the New Model Army was thus tied down, enabling the King to manoeuvre more freely. Elsewhere, news was encouraging for the Royalists. Leven was withdrawing, although he had captured Newcastle; Montrose had won yet another victory at Auldearn and the possibility that he would attempt to join the King was now a real one. In Wales, the Roundheads had been defeated by Charles Gerard at Newcastle Emlyn. Evesham fell on the 26th May, however, and Sir Edward Nicholas told the King that the city of Oxford was not in fact as well provided for as he had expected. It was necessary to lure Fairfax away. Reinforced by Langdale's Northern horse and Lord Loughborough's local levies, the King decided to march on Leicester. A battery was erected and the town was summoned by Prince Rupert. The summons was refused and the town stormed. Fighting was fierce and the brutality of the Royalist victors in London was loudly proclaimed in London, although it was undoubtedly much exaggerated. The fall of Leicester rendered the Eastern Association vulnerable, so Cromwell was sent to cover the area while Fairfax was ordered to prepare to march and Newport Pagnell was strengthened against the possibility of attack. The King's Council, as usual, was divided. Rupert continued to advocate that if the Royalists went on wreaking havoc in the Midlands, Fairfax would be forced to move north. Moreover, a thrust into Yorkshire, which was now completely unguarded, must bring the New Model Army in the wake of the Royalists.

While the King lingered at Daventry, the New Model Army collected with speed and efficiency. What was more, they had in their possession a letter from Goring, which had been intercepted, saying that he was unable to come to the King with the expected reinforcements. Forward elements of the New Model Army attacked the Royalists on the 12th June. They at once stood to arms on Burrow Hill, near Kislingbury, but they were ill-prepared and it was decided to draw back. The Roundheads pursued, harrying the Royalists until a Council called at Market Harborough decided to give battle. Rupert chose the site for the battle; a long ridge at Naseby to the south of Market Harborough from which he could dominate the New Model Army and threaten any move it might make. The going was good for horse, but the Royalists were outnumbered, as Fairfax had been reinforced by Cromwell on the 13th June.

	Royalists	*Roundheads*
Horse	5,200	
Foot	4,000	14,000
Dragoons	?	
Guns	?	

It is interesting that the Royalists at Naseby had more horse than foot; the ratio was normally reversed. There is no breakdown for the New Model Army but despite this, the Roundheads were certainly superior in cavalry. The two experienced forces drew up speedily. Rupert, on the Royalist right wing, faced Commissary-General Henry Ireton: Astley, commanding the Royalist foot, faced the numerically superior forces of Roundhead foot under Philip Skippon; Langdale, his forces well under strength, faced Cromwell. Fearing a repetition of Marston Moor, Rupert opened the battle by charging Ireton. The latter broke after some resistance but the impetus of the Royalist charge, as ever, took them on to the baggage train which was parked about half a mile behind the front line of the New Model. At the same time as Rupert charged, Astley also advanced with the foot. The disintegration of the Roundhead left should have allowed Rupert to attack Skippon's exposed flank, but his cavalry had met opposition in the form of the guard at the baggage train and unsuccessful attempts to capture it lost valuable time. Rupert himself rallied his men and brought them back to the field, but the horses were too tired to charge.

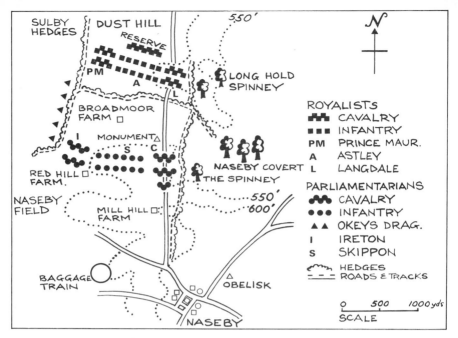

Battle of Naseby, 1645

The foot, meanwhile, although outnumbered, were fighting with dogged determination, and what is more, they were winning. Skippon had been wounded and as the morale of his troops wavered, so that of the Royalists seemed to take on a new lease of life. It was on the left wing that the action was most crucial. Langdale's dispirited and weakened force had not liked the idea of leaving the North in the first place. By the time they reached Naseby, they were mutinous. They were pitted against Cromwell's vastly superior horse, superior in both numbers and discipline. The action was brief, for although Langdale's men began with resolution, Cromwell's men were invincible. Having routed the northern horse, Cromwell sent a detachment to prevent them from rallying and himself attacked the rear of the Royalist foot. The King was an observer to all this and would have lead his guard to counter attack but at this point, an unknown member of his staff laid hold of his bridle and asked '*Will you go upon your death in an instant*?' Wheeling the King's mount away from Cromwell's pursuit, the Lifeguard that attended him followed and the whole party galloped from the field. The Royalist foot were now in a hopeless state, although there was a last stand in which a nucleus of regiments – including Rupert's Bluecoats – repulsed two cavalry charges before being overwhelmed. Fairfax himself took part in the action, killing an ensign and taking his colour. One last, co-ordinated attack saw the end of the Royalist Army which was then relentlessly pursued for 30 miles.

The King met Rupert and Maurice at Leicester. From there he made his way to Hereford to join with Charles Gerard and raise a new body of Welsh infantry.

* * *

In the west, the King's only remaining army, consisting of about 2,000 horse and 5,000 foot, was committed to the siege of Taunton. Goring reckoned that, once the town fell, he would be able to march his sizeable force to the aid of the King. Elsewhere, Byron, briefly given respite at Chester, was once again besieged by Sir William Bereton and Sir Thomas Middleton. Charles Gerard, although he had 3,000 foot under his command in Wales, was pitted against Massey's superior force. Despite the superiority of numbers against them, however, the Royalists could easily have joined the remnants of the Oxford army and the complete western force for, after Naseby, Fairfax went on to besiege Leicester which fell to him on the 18th June. Goring, sanguine, had reckoned that Taunton would not be a hard nut to crack, but he was wrong and opinion in London favoured the relief of Taunton, and Fairfax was ordered there with all speed. He took a southerly route since Royalist garrisons blocked a more northerly line of march. He had about 14,000 men which outmatched Goring's smaller force and he was reinforced by Massey en route. Goring, whose military habits had not endeared him to the local populace, raised the siege of Taunton as Fairfax approached and retired beyond the Rivers Parrett and Yeo. On his way, Fairfax had taken the precaution of pacifying the Dorset Clubmen, a group which adhered to neither side and wished only to be left in peace. The Royalists took up a position between Langport and Yeovil which met the van of Fairfax's army, advancing from Crewkerne. Goring's army fell back to the line of the Yeo between Langport and Yeovil, a long stretch to defend, but the Yeo was only fordable in places. The Roundheads concentrated at Crewkerne and sent a party to outflank the left wing of Goring's line, thus forcing the whole Royalist front to retire. The Royalists now concentrated around Langport but they were still outnumbered. Goring decided to try and force Fairfax to divide his army and he accordingly sent out a force under George Porter in a feint towards Taunton. Fairfax rose to the bait and sent a force after the Royalists. Although Porter was surprised and beaten near Ilminster, the odds against Goring were now reduced, and he decided to withdraw to Bridgwater, beginning on the 10th July when he sent his baggage and guns away. The Royalists covered their withdrawal from a strong position east of the town. Fairfax decided to assault the pass through which the Royalist artillery and baggage were moving. Roundhead artillery opened the battle and got the better of the light guns which was all the Royalists had left. The artillery duel was followed by the advance of 1,500 musketeers. After some skirmishing, the Roundhead horse formed up to charge across the ford of the Wagg Rhyne. The first wave was repulsed, but the Roundheads pressed home the attack and the Cavaliers

112

(2)

Sr beinge comanded by you to this
service, I thinke my selfe bound to ac-
quaint you with the good hand of God
towards you, and vs. wee marched ysterday
after the Kinge whoe went before vs
from Dauentree to Haureborow, and quartered about six miles from him, this day
wee marched towards him, Hee drew out
to meete vs. both Armies engaged. wee,
after 3. howres fight, very doubtfull
att last routed his Armie, killed and
tooke about 5000. very many officers:
but of what quallitye wee yett know
not, wee tooke alsoe about 200. carri-
all hee had, and all his gunns, beinge
12. in number, whereof 2 were demi
canon, 2. demi Culueringes, and (I
thinke) the rest sacres, wee pursued
enimie from three miles short of Ha-
to nine beyond, euen to sight of Leicer.
whether the Kinge fled, Sr this is non
other but the hand of God, and to him
aloane belongs the Glorie, wherein none
and to share with him, The Generall
serued you with all faythfullness. in
honor, and the best comendations I can
giue him is, [...] I doe, say hee

Austgust 14th. 1645.
Hauerborow.

your most humble servant
Oliuer Cromwell

The Battle of Naseby – Letter from Oliver Cromwell to William
Lenthall, Speaker of the House of Commons, written from Market
Harborough on the day of the battle

were finally defeated. Goring fell back to Bridgwater and thence into Devonshire. His army, if not annihilated, could not fight again, while the Roundhead position in the West was greatly strengthened.

*　　*　　*

The West, moreover, was the King's last hope for everywhere else, garrisons were falling. Bristol and Bridgwater were still in Royalist hands and it was decided to make the former city the headquarters for the next campaign. Charles was in Wales where he had had some hopes of raising a new army, but he found a poor response to his call. The local commander Gerard, had Goring's aptitude for alienating the local populace and recruitment was slow. In the north, however, there was a ray of hope, for Montrose was in the field and achieved yet another victory over the Covenantors at Alford on the 2nd July. Charles resolved to go to Scotland on the strength of this success. Rupert had misgivings about the wisdom of the decision, and in a letter to the Duke of Richmond, said so. The Prince was at Bristol, strengthening and fortifying it as best he could. He realised that the war was lost and advocated a treaty, an opinion that brought him into increasing conflict with Digby whose sanguine hopes of Irish reinforcements and a miraculous revival of the Royalist cause in the west never failed to charm the King's ear. As pockets of Royalist resistance were gradually eliminated in the west, Fairfax moved inexorably in on Bristol which was the last major threat in the West. The defences of the city were in poor repair and the garrison was undermanned. Supervising the preparations, Rupert must have known that a determined siege would be the end of the city. The townsfolk were hostile to the Royalists and even the garrison was not in good temper. Rupert wrote to his uncle in August saying that, if there was no mutiny, he could hold the city for four months in the event of a siege. His optimism was almost equal to that of Digby and the King. In September, the New Model Army closed in around Bristol and summoned the city. The summons was refused and on the 10th, the Roundheads attacked. The defences were in such bad shape that the outer ring presented little problem to the attackers. The Royalists, as the Round-heads had done two years before, retreated behind the inner ring of defences, but the situation was hopeless and Rupert's only choice lay between surrender or massacre. He surren-dered, after stalling for as long as possible, and obtained terms that were magnanimous indeed. The garrison marched out with bag and baggage and swords. They were even lent firearms by the victors for protection on the journey to Oxford for which they were given safe conduct. The fall of the King's last major port stunned him and provided the lever for which Digby had been waiting. His dislike of Rupert was veiled in anxiety for the King's welfare; he accused the Prince of trying to overthrow the King, and Charles was talked into believing that the Elector Palantine's presence in London and the powerful positions held by many of Rupert's close friends in the Army – notably Will Legge – were a direct threat to his throne. He dismissed Rupert, accusing him of surrendering Bristol 'basely'. He clearly believed what Digby told him; that Rupert had sold the town to Fairfax. Although the Prince was later cleared of these charges, he was never restored to military command and thereafter fought only as a volunteer, although he was given leave to raise a new Lifeguard early in 1646. The King moved north to Chester which was still threatened, and while he was there witnessed the battle of Rowton Heath where Colonel-General Sydenham Poyntz was defeated in a fierce fight on the 24th September.

In Scotland, Montrose had suffered a resounding defeat at

Philiphaugh where David Leslie fell on his small force and scattered it, massacring the Irish troops and their adherents. Montrose homself was with difficulty persuaded to flee the field, and to take to the heather.

*   *   *

The King, downcast by the defeat at Rowton Heath, moved to Newark. From here, Digby marched north with what troops could be spared, to join Montrose: the move was political rather than military since Rupert was on his way to the King to demand a court-martial and Digby had too much on his conscience to want to face the furious and bitter Prince. Digby's force joined Langdale's and both were defeated at Sherburn-in Elmet on the 15th October.

Civil War Infantry. Note the musketeer's bandlier of ammunition "the twelve apostles"

Elsewhere, Devizes, Winchester and Basing House fell, the latter having been a thorn in the sides of the Roundheads since the start of the war. It had been courageously held against two sieges and had succeeded in interrupting and harrying Parliamentary traffic between London and the west. The Prince of Wales tried to recoup what he could in Devon and Cornwall. Goring had gone abroad and his post had passed to Lord Wentworth, whose only talent lay in the bottle. On the 15th January, Hopton was made Commander in the West with Wentworth as his deputy. Meanwhile, Fairfax, having relieved Plymouth and taken Dartmouth, marched to Exeter which he besieged. Hopton's first action with the reorganised remnants of the Western Army, went to relieve Exeter. Fairfax left a brigade to threaten Exeter while he himself went after Hopton. The surrender of Chester to Bereton on the 3rd February had left the Northern Commander free to deal with the rest of the Royalist forces. Fairfax and Hopton met at Torrington and after a fierce contest, the Royalists were driven out of the town and pursued westwards. Their only consolation was the fact that heavy casualties had been inflicted on the enemy. The position in the west was now hopeless. Prince Charles sailed to the Scilly Isles on the 2nd March, Hopton surrendered his army on the 12th March and Exeter fell on the 9th April. Only Pendennis Castle held out.

Convinced at last that the Irish would not help him, the King now hoped for aid from France. The last remnants of his field forces, about 3,000 men under Lord Astley lay in Worcestershire, and were ordered to Oxford. On the way, they were caught and routed at Stow-in-the-Wold on the 20th March, and the last of the Royalist armies was destroyed. Except for isolated towns and castles, the Parliament was now all victorious. Charles, still negotiating with any and every source he could think of, surrendered himself to the Scots before Newark. The

117

Scots asked him to order the surrender of the garrison, which he did. He was then taken North despite the horrified protests of the Parliament at Westminster.

Oxford, under the governorship of Sir Thomas Glenham, was besieged in June. It surrendered on the 24th June and the last of the King's Court was permitted to leave honourably. Only Raglan, Pendennis and Harlech Castles now held out. Raglan and Pendennis fell during August. Harlech held out until the 13th March 1647, but the First Civil War was over long before then.

The King's supporters had been scattered but not eliminated, and although Charles himself and two of his children were prisoners, his son and heir was in France and it was there his followers now gravitated.

8. The Second Civil War

*"I ... conjure you to think seriously of the
difference there is in the choice you make, and I
doubt not you will choose what will be most
honourable and most just, and preserve and
defend the King whereto you are by oath
obliged."*

PRINCE OF WALES TO FAIRFAX

The First Civil War ended as rather an anti-climax. The King,
though defeated, was in the hands of the Scots and the victorious Parliament was becoming increasingly divided. In fact,
having got their victory, the Parliament was now unable to take
advantage of it for the breach between Presbyterians and Independents had widened. The Scots and the English continued to
try to come to terms with the King, but Charles stuck rigidly to
his principles and negotiations with the Scots foundered
because the introduction of Presbyterianism into England was
anathema to him. He had also rejected proposals submitted to
him from Parliament in July 1646. In the end, the Scots and the
English came to agreement whereby the Parliament would pay
their allies a long overdue sum for their aid in the war, in return
for which the King would be handed over to the Parliament.
The transaction duly took place and the King, encouraged by
the division in the House, cheerfully negotiated with both sides
from his place of captivity at Holmby in Northamptonshire.

In London, the Parliament was making ready an expedition

to Ireland but it was facing serious pecuniary difficulties. In order to try and alleviate the difficulties, the Commons made the dangerous decision to disband the New Model Army – or those parts of it not needed for Ireland – without making good arrears of pay. As the Army had spent its time since the cessation of hostilities plundering and desecrating buildings all over the country, this course of action found favour with most civilians but the soldiers themselves were far from happy and Fairfax warned the Commons to beware of the temper of his troops. Cromwell, who served in the House and in the Army, teetered on the fence and contrived to indicate his preference for the latter by ordering the train of artillery at Oxford to be secured by Cornet Joyce who was then sent on to the captive King at Holmby. The action was correctly interpreted at Westminster and Cromwell wisely joined the Army in East Anglia. The King was taken to Hampton Court while the situation between Army and Parliament rose to a crisis. The Army set up a General Council which debated its grievances and presented the "Declaration of the Army" on the 14th June, saying that they would not disband without settlement of all political and financial debts. The Parliament took fright and called out the Trained Bands but there was a poor response and the defence of the city was left to an unruly band of erstwhile soldiers and apprentices. Parliament's handling of the Army's Declaration angered the mob who stormed the Commons and forced some members to join the Army, which was marching south. On the 6th August the Army entered London, but withdrew to Putney where the General Council continued to meet. Extreme factions within the Army, demanding Parliamentary reform, clashed with more moderate members who had advocated a limited Monarchy, biennial Parliaments and religious toleration. The General Council got so out of hand that it was broken up on the 11th November. That same day Charles escaped from

120

Hampton Court and went to Carisbrooke Castle where he began to treat with the Scots. He succeeded in reaching an agreement with them whereby he undertook to impose Presbyterianism on England, suppress the sectaries and to confirm the Covenant in Parliament in return for military aid which would restore him to the throne. When Parliament heard of the King's activities they broke off all negotiations with him and passed the vote of "No Addresses". Prior to this, even Cromwell had advocated negotiating with the King if his return would have meant the restoration of peace within the country. At this point, the Second Civil War broke out, prompted chiefly by the fact that no satisfactory settlement had arisen out of the First War but also by the actions of Republican extremists which had driven many moderates back to the King. Less politically, people outside London were suffering from the military committees set up by Parliament to raise funds and recruit troops; since the end of the war these committees had occupied themselves by sequestering Royalist estates and, in consequence, causing upset amongst those employed on them.

Fairfax and Cromwell acted separately for the risings were scattered and unco-ordinated. In many areas, the citizens did not revolt in support of the King so much as against Parliament and the Regional Committees, which in some cases imposed martial law on matters which were purely civil in origin. Four areas were involved in major military activity. These were Wales, Scotland, the North, and South-East.

Although there was some unrest in London, the first open declaration for the King took place at Pembroke Castle in Wales where Colonel Poyer refused to surrender the garrison until arrears of pay were paid. On the 23rd March 1648, however, he abandoned this line and declared for the King, an action which was swiftly emulated in South Wales. In the north, Langdale took the offensive and seized Berwick on the 28th

121

April, followed by Sir Philip Musgrave who took Carlisle on the 29th April. A month later, a Royalist rising occurred in Kent where Dartford, Deptford and Rochester were taken. At the same time the Fleet, – under the command of the unpopular extremist Colonel Rainsborough – mutinied in the Downs and the largely Presbyterian officers arrested some of their Independent colleagues. By the time the Parliament had reappointed Warwick as Lord High Admiral, the sailors themselves had landed to occupy the Downs forts and refused to obey their officers.

Meanwhile, the situation with Scotland had worsened and the Scots had demanded of Parliament, that all Englishmen take the Covenant, that the Vote of No Addresses be rescinded so that negotiations with Charles could be resumed, and that the New Model Army should be disbanded. These requests were refused and the Scots under the Duke of Hamilton prepared to invade England. The invasion would be in support of the Royalists, many of whom were not Covenanters and this fact caused a split between Hamilton's forces, and the clergy who were in turn supported by Argyll.

Although both the Scots and the Royalists found it hard to recruit from a population which, in general, had too recent an experience of war to want to embark on another one, the threat to the established Army of the Parliament was a real one.

Fairfax, now a Baron, having inherited his father's title, was faced with these immediate revolts and grumbling discontent in Essex and the West Country which could at any time erupt into rebellion. His army was much weaker than it had been at the end of the First Civil War since many units had been disbanded. Much of its strength was tied up in garrisons which had to be held and by the time other forces had been deployed to cover potential troublespots, Fairfax had only a small force left with which to deal with London and Kent. Cromwell was sent into

122

Wales to join Colonel Horton whose original task had been to see to the disbanding of General Laugharne's army. Fairfax, having quelled several outbreaks of violence in London during March and April, turned his attention to the Royalist uprising in Kent. This was led by the Earl of Norwich (George Goring's father) whose followers included rebellious seamen and Cavaliers but comparatively few local citizens who were reluctant to take part in a revolt which might lead to another war. Mustering at Hounslow Heath on the 27th May, Fairfax marched to Blackheath and thence to Eltham on 30 May, reaching Gravesend on the 31st May from where he was able to reconnoitre the town of Rochester which was too strongly held for his army to attempt to take it. Instead, therefore, Fairfax moved south via Malling, to Maidstone which was held by Norwich with 3,000 men. Outside the town, 7,000 more men, acting as a 'reserve' were encamped and 1,000 more secured the passage of the Medway at Aylesford. Fairfax crossed the Medway at Farleigh Bridge on the 1st June and his van clashed with the "reserve" outside Maidstone as soon as they arrived.

Infantry advance with levelled pikes

Fairfax had wanted to open the battle on the following day but he was compelled to engage as soon as the rest of his force came up. The Royalists put up a stiff resistance and fighting went on until after dark. When the soldiers under Fairfax's command gained entry to the town, Norwich's 'reserve' fled but the Earl himself managed to escape with 3,000 men. With these, he made for London, reaching Blackheath on the 3rd June. He seized Bow Bridge but was brought up short here when support expected from the City did not materialise. Faced with Skippon's Trained Bands, Norwich crossed the Thames to Essex where he made for Colchester. This town had risen on the 4th June when the county Committee had been seized by Colonel Henry Farr who commanded the local Trained Bands. The Essex insurgents were commanded by Sir Charles Lucas who was joined by Sir George Lisle, Lord Capel and Norwich. Fairfax crossed the Thames at Tilbury on the 11th June and his van was approaching Colchester by the 12th June while Lucas speedily rendered the town defensible although he was hampered by a shortage of arms; the magazine at Braintree had been seized by Parliamentarian Trained Bands. Fairfax advanced on the city hoping to take it as he had done Maidstone, but Colonel Barkstead, leading his brigade up the London Road, met a force of Royalist foot deployed across it, flanked by horse, and three successive assaults on this position were repulsed. Although the Royalist left wing of horse was routed, the Parliamentarians were unable to turn the flank of the Royalist foot and when Barkstead at last managed to penetrate the outer line of the defences, he was ejected almost immediately. Further attempts to storm the town were made on the following day, but they proved futile and Fairfax was forced to invest the place for a formal siege. This was untimely, for elsewhere the Parliamentarians were not faring at all well. Although Ireton had entered Canterbury and Rich had relieved Dover, and

124

reduced Deal and Walmer, while risings in the West, North Wales and the Midlands were put down, Cromwell was tied down before Pembroke and Lambert in the North was fully occupied by Langdale's activities. The latter had taken Pontefract Castle, thus tying Lambert to that area when he was also threatened by an imminent Scottish invasion. Added to which, the fleet, though partially secured by Warwick, was still mutinous and ten of the ships in the Downs had weighed anchor and sailed to Holland where they declared for the King.

*　*　*

The Scots army crossed the border into England on the 8th July. The force joined Musgrave and Langdale at Carlisle before continuing south to Penrith where Lambert had stationed himself.

In Surrey, a Royalist rising at Kingston, led by the Earl of Holland with, amongst others, the Duke of Buckingham and Lord Francis Villiers, marched on Reigate Castle. Fairfax sent a force under Sir Michael Livesey against the party. The Royalists fell back through Dorking but were caught at Ewell and scattered. Villiers was killed and Holland escaped only to be captured at St. Neots. In Essex, Colchester continued obdurate, but on the 11th July Pembroke surrendered to Cromwell, freeing him to march north to Lambert's aid.

Lambert himself retreated slowly before the advance of the Scots, for Hamilton was a dilatory commander and, although the two forces clashed outside Penrith, there was no major activity and the Scots did not seem to be disposed to march south immediately. A force from Ulster under Sir George Monro arrived at Kendal to join the Scots, but he quarrelled with the Earl of Callander, Hamilton's second-in-command, with the result that the Ulster groups remained inactive at Kirkby Lonsdale. It was reckoned by Lambert that Hamilton would march into Yorkshire to try and relieve Pontefract and Cromwell, marching north as fast as possible, came to the same conclusion. In fact, no such resolution had been made. The council was divided and it was finally decided to march into Lancashire where Royalist supporters were expected to join the force. There were fewer of these than might have been expected since the behaviour of the Scots served to alienate even the Lancashire Royalists. Although the Royalists outnumbered the Parliamentarians, their morale was low, food was short as was ammunition and artillery, and indeed the campaign had begun with no artillery at all. The lack of forage prompted Hamilton to allow wider dispersion of the force for ease of foraging with the result that when the horse reached Wigan on the 16th August, the foot was still 16 miles further north at Preston. At the same time, Cromwell was moving on Preston from Yorkshire where he had attacked Pontefract before joining Lambert at Wetherby. His aim was to attack Hamilton, if possible, in the Pennines or to fall on the Scots' flank as it marched through Lancashire. Either course would nullify the Scots' advantage of superior numbers – about 9,000 to 20,000 (the latter figure excluding Monro's force of 2,700 which was well behind the main body). Langdale was on the left flank of the advancing Royalist army, moving south from Settle along the Ribble valley. He was thus in the best position to be able to discern danger from the Yorkshire flank, but he did not see fit to impart his suspicions to Hamilton. Cromwell marched via Skipton, Gisburn and Clitheroe to Preston – an exact reversal of the route Rupert had taken to relieve York four years earlier – meeting the first Royalists at Clitheroe. The safest course for Cromwell to adopt was for him to place his force between Wigan and the Scots line of advance. Instead he chose to advance directly on Preston so that by the 16th August, Langdale's force was camped directly between the foot in Preston and Cromwell's men in Stonyhurst Park. When he told Hamilton of the fact, the Duke, prompted by Callander, inclined to the opinion that Langdale exaggerated the situation and made no effort to alert the rest of his scattered army.

Langdale began to retreat towards Preston on the 17th August, pursued by Cromwell. His rear guard was soon caught and attacked by the van of Cromwell's force and Langdale himself halted his main body 2 miles from Preston before going into the town himself to tell Hamilton what was going on. The Duke was forming his foot up ready to cross the Ribble and continue its southward march. Once again prevailed upon by Callander, he declined to offer Langdale any aid whatever and the latter, who must by then have known that he faced the whole of Cromwell's army, rode back to his troops with no alternative but to make a stand against the superior force. He deployed his men in enclosed ground unsuitable for cavalry, his forward positions being swiftly pushed back to the oncoming enemy. Cromwell, unaware of how unequal the numbers were, deployed his forces on a wider front than Langdale's. The fight did not begin until 4 p.m. due to the difficulty of the terrain and the consequent length of time it took Cromwell to deploy.

The Parliamentarian assault met with stiff resistance, particularly in the centre, but although Langdale's men fought bravely, they were gradually forced back by the weight of the attack. It was some time, however, before the Royalists began to retreat towards Preston, but as soon as the troops were clear of the enclosures, Cromwell's wide front was able to turn in on Langdale's narrower one, turning the retreat into a rout, which lasted right into Preston. The Duke of Hamilton, at last convinced that Langdale's fears had not been ill-founded, had ordered fresh troops and supplies of ammunition be sent to him. His foot was collecting on Preston Moor and it was here he proposed to give battle, having sent word to Middleton with the horse to come up with all speed. At this point, Callander once more intervened, advocating a withdrawal south of the river, there to

127

await the arrival of the horse and the better opportunity to give battle on more even terms. The Moor, he said, was too favourable to Cromwell's cavalry. Hamilton agreed to this plan, although he must have realised that its implementation meant the virtual abandonment of Langdale's force which was now being harried through Preston. The withdrawal was effected with two brigades holding the bridge against Cromwell's men. Hamilton was soon left on the Moor with only the rear guard, cut off from the bridge by the advance of the Parliamentarians who had disposed of most of Langdale's foot, his horse fleeing North. After several attempts, this party broke through the enemy and swam the river, swollen by the heavy rain which had done much to lower the morale of the Scots army. The bridge was held by the Scots until their forces were deployed along the Darwen, a tributary of the Ribble, but as soon as the Parliamentarians crossed the Ribble, they quickly took the bridge over the Darwen. By nightfall, part of Cromwell's force was over that bridge as well and had captured some Scottish wagons. Cromwell himself, anxious to bring the dispirited Scots to battle, posted his forces to make certain that his victim did not try to escape northwards. Hamilton, his force now depleted to the tune of 6,000 men of which 1,000 were killed and 5,000 captured, held another council of war. Once again, Callander's opinion prevailed and it was resolved to make a withdrawal under cover of darkness towards Middleton who was advancing north with the horse. The weather was appalling and the manoeuvre served only to lower morale still further. What was worse, the horse advancing from Wigan, had taken a parallel road to that along which the foot were trudging south. The forces consequently passed each other en route without realising it, and Middleton arrived at the Darwen as instructed only to find himself confronted by Cromwell's army. He beat a hasty retreat down the road the foot had taken, pursued by a small

128

body of horse which was followed up by the main body of Cromwell's force. After a fighting retreat, Middleton at last caught up with the foot who were drawn up on Wigan Moor. By now, the latter were desperately miserable, chronically short of ammunition and powder, most of the Reserve having fallen into Cromwell's hands, and were generally in no condition to fight. Although Hamilton still had slight numerical superiority, he knew his foot was in no condition to make a stand, and they marched off, via Wigan, towards Warrington, covered by the horse. As the last of the foot reached Wigan, Cromwell's van met Middleton's horse and in the ensuing melée, some of the Royalists broke and made a dash towards Wigan. Sir James Turner who commanded the Royalist rear guard of foot, made a stand in the market place to repel any enemy attack and when the Royalist horse appeared, his panic-stricken men refused to let them through, almost killing Turner himself. The fleeing horse was brought up short and Turner told them to charge the pikemen, that being the only way they would get through. The defensive posture of the brigade deterred them, but when the cry was sent up that Cromwell's horse approached, the Royalists charged their own men and got through, though many of the pikemen did not scatter as expected, but were mown down. Despite this episode, most of the Royalist horse stayed together and fell back through Wigan in good order.

The remains of the Royalist foot made a stand at the defensible defile at Winwick, three miles from Warrington. There was a fierce action during which the unknown Royalist commanding the force was slain. An estimated 1,000 men were killed and 2,000 captured before the force pulled back to Warrington which was to be fortified as soon as the remains of the Scots Army collected there. At this point Hamilton escaped with the horse – possibly on the advice of Callander whose exceptionally bad counsel had been largely responsible for the shattering defeat. Baillie, instructed to come to terms with Cromwell, did so, though he was personally reluctant to capitulate. Cromwell found himself with more prisoners than soldiers, but guarding the Scots was not much of a problem as the hostility of the countryside discouraged escape. Hamilton continued south, for Lord Byron had risen – unsuccessfully as it happened – in Cheshire and he hoped to join him with the remains of his army which now consisted of 4,000 horse and foot. The Scots were thoroughly humiliated and Middleton was captured at Stone in Staffordshire. Hamilton surrendered at Uttoxeter (he was later tried and executed by the Lords). Langdale made a temporary escape with some Horse, but was captured at Nottingham. Callander and Monro both got away, the former to Holland, the latter to Scotland. The last remnants of the northern Royalists capitulated at Appleby.

Following the collapse of the Royalist offensive in the North, Colchester surrendered on the 28th August. The terms were harsh but this was not due so much to the fact that the town had carried out a stubborn and courageous defence for ten weeks as to the attitude of the Parliament to the Royalist rebels who were not regarded as fellow soldiers so much as insurgents. Soldiers and officers below the rank of Captain had quarter for their lives, but the others were at the mercy of Fairfax. Of these, Lisle, Lucas and Sir Bernard Gascoigne were sentenced to death. Gascoigne as an Italian, was reprieved, but Lisle, and Lucas were both shot. The action is still the subject of controversy. The capitulation of Colchester more or less ended the Second War. In Scotland, the divided factions which had accompanied the raising of the Army now rose in revolt. In the Wiggamore Raid, the Presbyterians under Lord Eglintar marched on Edinburgh and defeated Hamilton's supporters, led by his brother the Earl of Lanark. Argyll took power once more and Cromwell, who had followed Monro north, met him, and agreed to give him military aid in return for Berwick and Carlisle. The exchange agreed, Cromwell moved south to besiege Pontefract Castle. Meanwhile, the Commons had repeated the "Vote of No Addresses" as soon as they heard of the victory at Preston. The move was led by the Presbyterians and those who were in dispute against the army. Charles negotiated in order to spin out time but when he flatly rejected the treaty offered to him on the 16th November even the moderates lost patience with him. The Council of Officers approached the King but to no avail and, in the end, a Remonstrance was put before Parliament by the Army advocating that he be brought to trial.

Execution of Charles I

The lack of interest shown by Parliament in the implementation of the Remonstrance induced the Army to act. Charles's guards, from local regiments, were replaced by soldiers from the New Model on the 29th November and the following day he was taken from the Isle of Wight to Hurst Castle on the mainland. The army now announced its intention of marching to London and dissolving Parliament by force, creating a new one with Independents only. The situation was further exacerbated when the Presbyterians declared on the 5th December that the King's refusal of the treaty yet contained elements on which further negotiations could be based. On the 6th December Colonel Pride purged the Commons, relieving the Trained Bands which guarded it with his own men; 240 members were denied entrance to the House. Cromwell arrived in London that evening, with no intention of negotiating with Charles. Although Fairfax opposed what he saw coming, he could not divert the Council of Officers from their course.

Further attempts to come to terms with Charles on Christmas Day failed. On the 6th January, it was decided to try the King for *'High Treason and other high crimes.'* He was found guilty and condemned to death *'by the severing of his head from his body.'* Charles was duly executed on the 30th January outside the Banqueting Hall in Whitehall.

The monarchy was immediately abolished in England and a Council of State created. In Scotland, however, there was no such radical reformation and on the 5th February, Charles, Prince of Wales, was proclaimed King of Scotland.

From Holland, the new King viewed his kingdom: Scotland where his welcome was lukewarm and came with a list of provisos. Ireland where revolt was rife, and finally England where to pronounce his name was treason. It was a grim state of affairs.

9. Dunbar and Worcester

Fairfax: *"My lords, you will give me leave with all freedom to say to you that I think it doubtful whether we have a just cause to make an invasion upon Scotland"*
Cromwell: *"... they have invaded us, as your lordship knows ... since the national covenant and contrary to it, in that action of Duke Hamilton, which was by order and authority from the Parliament of that kingdom and so the act of a whole nation."*

King Charles II could have gone about regaining his throne in one of three ways. He could have pursued a diplomatic course, relying on foreign help and oblique military aid from countries concluding treaties with the new Republic; he could invade England and take his throne by force from Scotland or, lastly he could invade from Ireland.

On the 13th August 1649 Cromwell was able to set sail for the latter country where the Marquis of Ormonde had led a revolt which ousted Parliamentarians from all towns except Dublin and Londonderry. Favourably disposed to Charles though the Irish might prove to be, Cromwell's determined campaign, which was to encompass the actions at Rathmines and Drogheda, ruled out any possibility of Charles launching an invasion from that country.

In Scotland, however, Montrose had been created Lieutenant Governor of the country and Captain-General of all its forces by Charles II. While Scottish commissioners visited Charles in the Netherlands and sought to force him to take the

Covenant and to impose it on all his lands, Charles sent Montrose to Scotland in the hope that victory over the Covenanters would free him from the necessity to accede to these demands. On the 23rd March 1650, Montrose landed in the Orkneys with a force of German and Danish mercenaries. Urry secured the Ord of Caithness and this enabled Montrose to march into Sutherland where he recruited Highlanders to his cause. On the 12th April, Montrose crossed the Pentland Firth and took Thurso and Dunbeath Castle. Via the Ord, Montrose tried to take Dunrobin Castle, but when it refused to surrender, he moved on to Lairg and then to the Kyle of Sutherland where he awaited the promised reinforcements. Colonel Strachan was ordered by Leslie to concentrate the Covenanting Army in order to halt Montrose. The Covenanters at Brechin lured Montrose from his position at Carbisdale and his small force was then attacked and destroyed at once. Although Montrose himself escaped, he was later captured, along with Urry, who had already changed sides twice, and they were both hanged in Edinburgh on the 21st May.

The complete defeat of his last hope virtually forced Charles into taking the Covenant and this he did on the 23rd June 1650. Charles now went to Scotland and began to discuss the proposed invasion of England with Leslie. In fact, plans had been prepared before Charles took the Covenant, and while the Scots raised their army, the Council of State in England were able to foresee the threat and to set about countering it. It was proposed to invade Scotland on the strength of their aggressive intentions but Fairfax could not be persuaded that this was a right or lawful course of action, as the Scots were still their allies. Along with Cromwell, Fairfax was appointed to command this army which was to invade Scotland, but he was adamant about his decision: he would fight if the Scots invaded England, but not if England were to take the offensive in

134

Scotland. The deadlock was resolved when Fairfax resigned his command on the 26th June. Cromwell was now left in sole command.

Most of the New Model Army was engaged in the Scottish campaign. Cromwell's second-in-command was Fleetwood, while Lambert commanded the Horse and Monck the Foot. The danger of Royalist risings in England was still present, so some units were posted in major towns and local militia was called out. Meanwhile, Cromwell's army, which consisted of about 5,000 horse and 10,000 foot, arrived at Berwick on the 19th July. Leslie's army was large but mainly inexperienced. The Scots policy of not allowing any 'Engagers' to fight, i.e. those who had adhered to Hamilton and the "Engagement" he had signed with Charles I – meant that a large body of willing and able men were precluded from taking part in the war. With this force, Leslie took up a position which stretched from Leith to Edinburgh, covering the capital from the route by which Cromwell was most likely to advance. The area had been cleared of all fodder and forage which meant that Cromwell would have to be supplied by sea, and the only port of any size along the coast was Dunbar.

Cromwell advanced into Scotland on the 22nd July, reaching Dunbar on the 26th July. Here he received supplies from the fleet before moving on to Haddington. Lambert was then sent on to Musselburgh to see if it were possible to surprise the Scots. On the 29th July, Cromwell drew his army up to face Leslie, but it was immediately apparent that the Scots' defences were so strong that frontal assault would be impossible. In appalling weather conditions, the English army began to pull back towards Musselburgh. The withdrawal was fast and none too coherent. Lambert, commanding the rear guard, became separated from the main body and was promptly attacked by two bodies of Scots horse. The first Scottish charge drove in the rear, but then the rest of the English line stood and brought up fresh troops. In the ensuing skirmish Lambert himself was first wounded, captured and then rescued but in the end the Scots were routed, leaving the English to retire unmolested. Having reached Musselburgh, however, Cromwell was again attacked by a body of Scots horse under Major General Robert Montgomery. The English outposts were again driven in, but the Scots were eventually beaten off with loss. The port of Musselburgh is not as sheltered as that at Dunbar and it proved impossible to land supplies there. Cromwell was therefore forced to fall back to Dunbar once more, by which time, his army's strength had been lowered by between 4,000 and 5,000 men due chiefly to sickness.

The ultimate English objective was Edinburgh, and in order to draw the Scots from their strong position, Cromwell had to force them to give battle, despite the weakness of his own army. His new plan was to outflank Leslie's right wing and march to the Firth of Forth, whence, with the aid of the fleet, he could cut Leslie's lines of communication. Leslie, however, shadowed Cromwell and when the two armies met, Leslie's force was deployed behind a bog, giving Cromwell no hope of being able to attack. He retired yet again to Musselburgh, and thence to Dunbar, having been completely outmanoeuvred. Leslie followed the retreat but allowed the English to reach Dunbar on the 1st September. While Cromwell deployed his troops to cover their position, Leslie moved to cut the only road leading into Dunbar, placing his foot on Doon Hill, to the west of the road and his horse between the road and the sea. Cromwell now had the choice of giving battle and fighting his way out, or evacuating his army by sea. As the Scots finished their deployment on the 2nd September, it became evident to the English that Leslie meant to attack them for he had drawn his forces with artillery up on the lower slopes of Doon Hill and had

136

attacked Cromwell's outposts near the Broxburn, east of Dunbar. Leslie, it seems, had assumed that Cromwell had already begun to evacuate his army, though in fact he had done nothing of the kind. Leslie's attacking posture was less well adapted to defence and of this fact the English were well aware.

The numbers in the opposing forces, as far as can be established were as follows: English, 11,000 men, including over 3,000 horse and Scots, 22,000 men, including 6,000 horse. Both sides possessed adequate but unspecified amounts of artillery.

Despite Cromwell's lack of numbers, he decided to attack the

John Lambert

137

Scots before they were ready to deliver their assault. The English formed up on the Berwick Road near Broxmouth House, but the weather during the night was so bad that their dispositions took longer than expected and the Scots, after two false alarms, had decided that their attack would be impossible and retired to get what rest they could. Lambert and Fleetwood, with the majority of the horse and some of the foot, then attacked the Scots horse north of the Berwick Road. Their assault took the enemy completely by surprise, many troopers being caught under their tents when the English slashed the guy ropes. The superiority of Scots' numbers enabled them to put up an effective resistance, however. Monck attacked on the right, leading his foot against the Scots who were not only sodden and uncomfortable, but ill-prepared, their bunched, offensive deployment such as it was, being unsuitable to withstand the English onslaught. Despite their difficulties, the Scots held their position all along the front until the English reserve, under Pride and Overton, was brought against the centre by Cromwell. Attacking between Lambert and Monck, Cromwell's horse assaulted the Scots horse on the right and, cutting it off from the foot, brought about the collapse of that entire wing which turned tail and fled towards Berwick. Having disposed of this body, Cromwell turned his attention to the Scottish foot on the left which had, until now, held its own against Monck's forces. The English horse's flanking attack was fatal. The line was rolled up and most of the foot was scattered. The only two regiments which remained fought on until they were more or less destroyed. This part of the action had taken only an hour, but the English pursued their beaten opponents and in the course of the chase, the Scots army was annihilated, 3,000 men were killed and over 10,000 were captured. English losses were low, being only about 40.

While Leslie gathered together what remnants of his army he

could – these numbered between 4,000 and 5,000 – and retreated to Stirling, Cromwell marched to Edinburgh where the Castle held out against him. The English then marched on Stirling, but found that it was held too strongly to attack and they therefore returned to Edinburgh.

*   *   *

Charles II was by now in Perth. The action at Dunbar was not undertaken on his behalf, and had done little for the military reputation of the Covenanting Army, and he now strove to procure an agreement with the dour Covenanters whereby Royalists and Engagers would be allowed to fight in the Scots Army. It was largely Leslie's shattering defeat which strengthened Charles' position sufficiently for him to be able to obtain this agreement. Leslie himself had already begun to recruit Highlanders from his Stirling base, men who were not of the Covenant but whose martial capabilities were more promising than those of the previous army. Charles, employing every political expedient known to man, contrived to convince Argyll and the Covenanters of his good intentions and was crowned King of Scotland at Scone on the 1st January 1651.

Elsewhere in Scotland, anti-English feeling produced a series of raids which were a source of continual annoyance to Cromwell. Elements of his army were detached to deal with these thorns in the corporate side of the council-of-war and in February, goaded beyond endurance by Leslie's continual activity from Stirling, Cromwell himself advanced once more on the city only to be forced back, as before, by the appalling weather conditions. At this point, Cromwell caught a fever from which he did not recover until June. In England, it had become apparent that the campaign would be a protracted one and reinforcements were consequently sent North. The opposing side was also swelling in numbers with equal rapidity now that the act forbidding Engagers to enlist had been repealed by the Scottish Parliament. By the time Cromwell was fit again, the Royal Army, commanded by the King, with Leslie as second in command, and Middleton as Commander of the horse, was in a position to offer battle. Leslie left Stirling and marched on Torwood. Cromwell, from Linlithgow, sought to draw Leslie from this strong position there but the latter refused to move and Cromwell considered the place too strong to attack. Leslie had a total strength of perhaps 15,000 foot and 6,000 horse. From Linlithgow, Cromwell now made a feint towards Glasgow which Leslie resolutely ignored; he then stormed Callander House which likewise produced no response, forcing the English to adopt yet another plan of attack. This was to cut Leslie's supply line from Perth, where Charles' Government lay. While Cromwell screened Leslie's army at Torwood, a force was sent to begin the flanking movement but a force of Royalists shadowed them, until English reinforcements forced them to pull back. Lambert commanded the Parliamentary troops and he attacked the retreating force which was severely cut up in a fierce fight. When Cromwell further reinforced Lambert, Leslie resolved to take his entire army to Inverkeithing to attack the English, but Cromwell shadowed him closely, thus thwarting his design and forcing him to retire again to Stirling. The Scots army was now safe, but communications were gradually cut as Cromwell closed in, finally investing Perth on the 31st July. Leslie could now either turn and attack the beleaguering force to try and reopen his supply lines, or he could march into England recruiting troops as he went. Although Leslie favoured the former plan, Charles opted for the second and as the Royalists moved south on the 1st August, the English on both sides made ready to receive them. Cromwell, however, remained at Perth where he took the surrender of the city on the 2nd August. Sending forces to Stirling he ordered Lambert to harry

140

the advance of the Royalist Army and by the 5th August, Lambert was in a position to attack the rear of the enemy force while Harrison was to concentrate on the flank to the east. As the army prepared to meet the invaders as they had done Hamilton's army in 1648, the militia and trained bands were called out to aid them in their efforts.

The Royalists were relying heavily on recruits being picked up on route, but dissent between the Scots and the English within the army produced an ambivalent form of propaganda, the Presbyterian Massey being exhorted by the Covenanters who sought to force the full weight of their belief on adherents and thus merely succeeded in frightening them off. Crossing the border on the 6th August, Charles moved quickly south, reaching Wigan by the 15th August. The Earl of Derby joined the King there with some men recruited in the Isle of Man. He was sent off to his own territories in Lancashire in order to bring in further recruits, but the response there was poor and on the 25th August, a force under Lilburne defeated the Royalist recruits, Derby being seriously wounded during the melée.

Pikemen

The indifference of the success of recruitment helped to lower morale in the divided ranks of the Royalist Army. The Scots were dejected, and got continually more so as the Royalists moved south; Leslie himself was convinced that any action would result in a repetition of Dunbar and persisted in putting the worst possible complexion on events while his more sanguine commander-in-chief was able to admire the fine array of his army.

Charles' original intention had been to march on London. By the time he reached Warrington it had become evident that this move would be impossible and he accordingly resolved to continue down through the Western Counties in order to find a suitable place where his army might rest and recruit. Shrewsbury refused his summons and the army moved on to Worcester. A party of Royalists under Massey secured the bridge over the Severn at Upton, but were beaten off by Lambert, Massey being wounded during the engagement. The Parliamentarians now had freedom to manoeuvre on both sides of the Severn and Cromwell set about utilising this freedom as best he could. The Royalists still held a strong position, south of Worcester, along the River Teme which flows into the Severn from the west and thus prevented Cromwell from attacking up that side. In the area around Worcester the Royalists held the bridge over the Severn and so had complete freedom of movement between the city and the Teme. From his position, south of Charles' force, Cromwell took stock.

*   *   *

The Royalists were now heavily outnumbered, having only about 12,000 men to Cromwell's 25,000 to 30,000. Cromwell's numerical superiority enabled him to devise a two-pronged attack on his outnumbered opponents, to be launched on the first anniversary of the battle of Dunbar, 3rd September 1651.

142

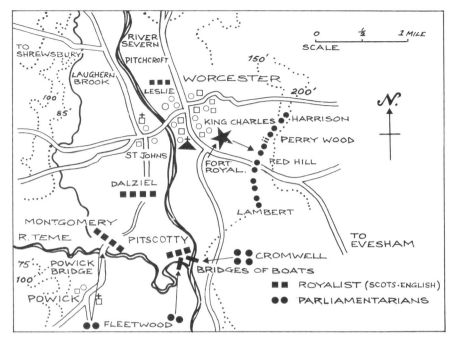

Battle of Worcester, 1651

The plan was to send a force into the east side of Worcester while Fleetwood attacked northwards, forcing crossings of the Teme, whence he would be able to swing west and assault Worcester from that direction. In support of Fleetwood, Cromwell was to send a supplementary force across a bridge of boats south of the confluence of the Teme and Severn, while he himself pressed home the eastern attack. Fleetwood advanced in two columns, the left hand (western) one marching on Powick Bridge, the other on the bridge of boats over the Teme just west of the confluence of the two rivers. The advance was slow since the men were held back by the need to keep pace with the boats, moving up the Severn, from which the bridges were to be made. As the men reached the Teme, they engaged Royalist musketeers on the north bank while, east of the Severn, Cromwell was constructing a bridge of boats across which he sent

143

reinforcements as soon as it was complete. By this time Fleetwood, too, had forced a crossing of the Teme and was advancing in strength, although the Royalists under Montgomery contested every foot of ground. On the west bank of the Severn, at St. Johns, Charles viewed the way the battle was running from the tower of Worcester Cathedral, and saw that Cromwell had committed most of his horse to fight on his left wing, and so resolved to use his own cavalry, still intact, against the prong of the attack threatening Worcester from the east. Covered by artillery from Fort Royal, the Royalists attacked south-east from Sudbury Gate towards the forces drawn up on Red Hill and beat them back until the militia, with whom they had engaged, were reinforced by regulars and troops from the fight on the west of the city. Fighting was fierce for about three hours, after which the Royalist horse broke and fled, pursued through Worcester by the victors who turned the guns of Fort Royal on the fugitives. Although the horse was able to escape, the foot, defeated on the west, had no alternative but to surrender; between 6,000 and 7,000 prisoners were taken that day and those that escaped northwards were ruthlessly hunted down. Leslie, Derby, Massey and Middleton were all captured and Charles himself was only able to escape by doffing his armour and slipping away unnoticed while a diversion was created. After a tense and nerve-racking journey through England, the King managed to take ship for France. For nine years he was to remain in exile, the hope for his Restoration being kept alive by a small, but determined, band of Royalists in his own country. His military power had been wrecked by the combined effects of three civil wars. Not only that, but the campaigns of Cromwell in England and Monck in Scotland saw to it that, by 1652, no place was left for the King to use as a base, should he contemplate any further attempt to regain his throne by force.

144

10. The Protectorate and Restoration

*"I have not been able to find it in my duty to
God & you to undertake this charge under that
title."*
CROMWELL, ON BEING OFFERED THE CROWN.

Parliament had finally won the Civil War and crushed the
opposition beyond hope of recovery but the complex causes of
the war made a comprehensive peace difficult to achieve. The
end of the First War in 1646 had produced a legislative hiatus
and this situation persisted as divisions within Parliament made
a political solution impossible, and then the intervention of the
Scots necessitated the drawing of a military conclusion. Sooner
or later, however, it was obvious that the fundamental causes of
the war would have to be dealt with and chief among these was
the question of the form of Government by which England was
to be ruled. The Monarchy and the House of Lords no longer
existed and the country was governed by the Council of State
and the Rump of the "Long Parliament", a stop-gap arrange-
ment which, if due only to internal strife, could not last.

Quite apart from the political and religious problems that
remained unsolved, the economy was in a precarious state,
having been subjected to a severe and protracted drain on its
resources by the Wars. Trade was at a standstill, and almost the

only income was derived from those Royalists fined for their allegiance to the Stuarts. For this reason, the Act of Indemnity, passed in 1652, which pardoned those who had committed 'treason' by adhering to the King before Worcester, was accompanied by a comprehensive list of exceptions which thus ensured a trickle of income to the impoverished Treasury.

By far the greatest power in the kingdom, however, was the army. The body that had been raised and organised to crush the Scots and Royalists now numbered something over 50,000 and was going to be a potent argument during the debate as to who or what would rule the country. But the army, too, was divided. Its three main factions saw the army as performing widely different functions. Harrison viewed it as the instrument of legal and religious reform, Lambert as the means by which England could be brought back to a more conservative method of government, headed by 'natural leaders', extremists like Ludlow as the path to setting England in the way of a republican state. On one thing these men were all agreed: the army would continue in existence, despite the evident opposition of the Rump, and the men would get their arrears of pay.

*   *   *

Within the army, the Rump was universally unpopular and when it sought merely to perpetuate itself in a slightly modified form by introducing and debating the "*Bill for a New Representative*," both extremes of the Army, for whom Cromwell provided a buffer, petitioned the General to take some action. Officers and some Members of Parliament agreed to delay the Bill and to discuss a different form of government, to be set up on a provisional basis. The decision was taken on the 19th April 1653. On the following day, the Rump took no notice of the resolution and proceeded with their Parliamentary business. They were interrupted by Cromwell who marched into the

146

House and informed his colleagues that as they were not accomplishing anything worth while, he proposed to dissolve the Parliament. The entrance of Harrison with some musketeers lent weight to his assertion. Speaker Lenthall was forcibly removed from his chair and the mace was taken away. Parliament was, indeed, dissolved. The Council of State went the same way in the afternoon, and the army was left in control of the kingdom.

It was evident that the Rump would have to be replaced, but the multitude of radicals and extremists produced a compromise Parliament, an appointed assembly which, however, was united enough to introduce measures so extreme that the moderates became seriously alarmed. This Parliament – a self-voted title for there were no elections – came to be known as the "Barebones Parliament" for one of its most radical and vociferous members was one Praise-God Barbon. As the year went on, the conservative faction in the Army, led by Lambert and supported by Cromwell, gained support from the gentry and middle-classes. Before the "Barebones Parliament" dissolved itself in December, Lambert and his followers had drawn up the Instrument of Government which laid down a new Constitution whereby the Kingdom was to be ruled by a Protector who had under him only one House. At the time it was put forward the "Barebones Parliament" took little notice of it, but after its dissolution, Lambert brought the question up again. On the 16th December, Cromwell accepted the title of Lord Protector and immediately incurred the wrath of the extremists. Some, like Harrison, refused to continue in the army and others, as typified by the *Petition of the Three Colonels*, objected that Cromwell now wielded more effective power than the monarch had done. Alteration of the franchise shifted the weight of representation in the House towards the growing urban middle-classes – merchants and tradesmen – but the Parliament, which met in September 1654, had an executive council composed largely of high-ranking army officers above it which formed the Protector's cabinet and as this body virtually controlled the 30,000-man army, Parliament found itself unable to bring any pressure to bear on the Council. The Parliament itself was divided; elections had returned at least 100 of the purged members and the two extremes remained in the House. The Republicans and the Royalists, (for a few of the latter had been elected) both hated Cromwell with a vehemence which arose from different springs of dissatisfaction. If the whole House was united on one issue, the disbanding of the large, and, to them, useless army, it was the one issue on which they could not hope to win. This Parliament, called the 'Healing and Settling' body, was dissolved in January 1655 unable to agree even on modifications of the Parliamentary Reform as laid down in the Instrument.

*　*　*

Cromwell, left in sole charge with only his Army Council to support him, turned his attention to more distant problems. He had managed to conclude peace with the Dutch in April 1654 after a short and unpopular war. Now he turned his hand to a more risky diplomatic problem. France and Spain were at war and Cromwell had thus far avoided committing England to the hostilities but when the Protector asked for trading concessions from Spain in the West Indies and was refused, he sent a British expedition to the Caribbean which, under Admiral Penn and General Venables, failed to effect a landing on Hispaniola in April 1655. Returning to their base in Jamaica, the English found that their force was so depleted by sickness that they were forced to abandon their design. Penn and Venables, who entertained a lively mutual hostility, were both confined to the Tower on their return from the disastrous expedition. Meanwhile, in England, the Protector was beset by other problems.

148

The Royalists, who now had no military resources to speak of, were still a threat to him for their design was to unite with all those factions – including Levellers and Dissenters – who were disenchanted with Cromwell. There had been an assassination attempt on the Protector in May 1654, but there was little chance for the planning and execution of a coup of this sort for Cromwell's spies, headed by the brilliant John Thurlor, were vigilant and effective. In January 1655, a plot to distribute arms was uncovered and, following the arrests which ensued, Cromwell banned race meetings and confiscated horses and powder from those suspected of complicity. The Royalists also suffered a set-back when they were unable to engage the full co-operation of the Levellers and Presbyterians, but they optimistically went on with their plans for revolt.

*   *   *

The "Risings" were to take place in different parts of the country, and synchronisation was almost impossible. Two men from the court of Charles II, then at Cologne, travelled to England to aid their fellows. Sir Joseph Wagstaffe landed in London and travelled to the south-west, an area which had generally supported Charles I during the First Civil War, while the Earl of Rochester – formerly Lord Wilmot – landed in the north.

The 8th March was the date set for the Risings, but although a few parties mustered, they had so little faith in the reliability of their counterparts who were to rise elsewhere that they soon filtered home again, having accomplished nothing. Wagstaffe had been campaigning amongst the gentry in Hampshire and Wiltshire and what success he achieved was largely dissipated by the fact that when, on the 11th March, the Royalists had plucked up sufficient courage to undertake the insurrection, the Hampshire levies were so late at their rendezvous that they had no hope of meeting the Wiltshire levies at Salisbury as planned.

149

Notwithstanding this, Colonel John Penruddock took 200 horse into the city before daylight and managed to seize horses, open the jails and capture the High Sheriff and the judges of Assize. Wagstaffe was dissuaded by Penruddock from hanging the Sheriff an act, he claimed, which would encourage the many Royalists in the area to show their hand. The Hampshire levies still had not arrived, but with their ranks swollen to between 300 and 400, Wagstaffe left Salisbury after proclaiming Charles II and marched west towards the traditional stronghold of the Royalists. They reached South Molton in Devon before they encountered serious opposition in the form of a troop of horse from Exeter, commanded by Captain Unton Crook. Here, on the 14th March, there was a short, sharp fight in which the Royalists were defeated and scattered. Wagstaffe was among those who escaped, hidden by local sympathisers until it was safe for him to travel abroad once more. Penruddock asked for quarter but once captured was later beheaded at Exeter while many of his followers were hanged at Salisbury. Others were transported to the Barbadoes as slaves.

* * *

In the north Rochester arrived full of resolution, but in Yorkshire the situation was no better than it had been in the south. The date for the Rising had been mistaken and by the time Rochester landed, most of the Royalists had given up and gone home. The insurrection came to nothing and those who persevered long enough to meet Rochester beset him with queries and problems which convinced all concerned that any attempt to persist in the design was folly. Rochester, sanguine as ever, travelled south in a leisurely fashion, and was nearly captured at Aylesbury but escaped to London and thence back to the King at Cologne.

150

While it is unlikely that, even had the Royalists succeeded in gaining the aid of a powerful body like the Presbyterians, the insurrection would actually have overthrown the Commonwealth, their dismal failure certainly strengthened Cromwell's position and enabled him to disband about 10,000 men from the New Model. The reduction in the strength of the Army eased the financial burden on the impoverished Exchequer, but the danger of further Risings remained and it was necessary to devise a means of keeping control of the country in a way that would be administratively simple and therefore cheap to operate. On the 31st October, Cromwell divided the country into twelve districts over each of which was a Major General or *'Bashaw'* who was to preside. Recalcitrant subjects were liable to have their estates confiscated and their activities reported to the Protector who would then decide any further action. The Major-Generals had military backing in the form of troops of horse and the local militia; their decisions were therefore usually incontrovertible if only because might overcame right. The upkeep of this system was funded by the proceeds of the Decimation Tax which fined the Royalists – whether they had taken part in the recent risings or not – one tenth of their estate. As many of them had compounded or been exempted by the Act of Oblivion, complaints were numerous. The usual response was coercion: Whalley responded to one man's complaint by quartering 50 men on him and threatening him with another 500 if he didn't pay. The Major-Generals were Puritans and they executed a policy whose chief aim was to make sure that everyone lived in a world as cheerless as they did, even if they were unable to reach as far as the conscience or soul of their victims. Royalists were forced to give security for the good behaviour of themselves and their servants, but the bonds were set at sums quite out of proportion to their means. The arguments put forward against payment of them smacked strongly

151

Volley firing by musketeers

of those put forward in opposition to the taxes levied by Charles I before the wars. The wheel was coming full circle.

Meanwhile, Cromwell was still dabbling in international diplomacy. Following his unsuccessful attack on Hispaniola, he sent Blake, now an Admiral, to harry Spanish treasure ships in the hope that the coffers of the Exchequer might benefit. Blake attacked both ships and colonies until the Spanish were goaded beyond endurance and declared war on the English. Money was needed for this development and Cromwell was thus forced to call a Parliament which met on the 17th September 1656. Although the Major-Generals had assured the Protector that no one hostile to him would be elected, 100 members were excluded from the first sitting. Despite this, Parliament was not compliant. £400,000 was voted for the Spanish war after news of the capture of £600,000 of Spanish treasure arrived in England, but beyond this, Cromwell was defeated on important issues. The Protector advocated religious toleration but the Parliament arrested, mutilated and

152

imprisoned a Quaker. The Militia Bill, providing for the continuation of the Decimation Tax, was thrown out. Extremists outside Parliament were also active. Charles II offered a knighthood and reward to anyone who could assassinate Cromwell and a former Leveller, Miles Sindercombe, planned to blow up Whitehall Chapel and Cromwell with it. Parliament's horror at this outrage, despite their opposition to Cromwell's measures, was genuine. In their expressions of congratulation on the avoidance of his fate, the House also suggested obliquely that he should assume the title of King. A more formal document, the Humble Petition and Advice, was introduced by Sir Christopher Pack on the 23rd February. Although the Army and extremists – particularly the Levellers – were opposed to it, the majority of the Parliament were in favour and although the debates were hot, the measure was passed and handed to Cromwell for his approval.

The document modified the constitution so that, in effect, he would be King, with the power to name his successor, choose the members of a new Upper House and manage a revenue of £1,300,000, although Parliament would decide how this money was to be raised. Parliament itself was strengthened by a clause which stated that no members were to be excluded unless it was by the consent of the House. Cromwell hesitated over the title of King, however. For several days he wavered then, persuaded by military colleagues that the army would not continue to support him if he became King he declined the title and the document was amended and passed on the 25th May, to be followed a month later by the Additional Petition and Advice. On the 26th June, the Protector was installed in a ceremony very similar to that of a coronation.

Cromwell had been making overtures to Sweden, in the hope of forming a Protestant Alliance, but his fleet was so heavily committed in the West Indies that he dared not risk an additional war in the Baltic. Instead, he signed a commercial treaty with Sweden in July. The war with Spain continued to run on satisfactorily until Charles signed a treaty with Philip IV of Spain which enabled him to raise an army in the Spanish Netherlands. This force grew so rapidly that it became an obvious threat to the Commonwealth. In order to halt this menace, Cromwell contracted an alliance with France whereby he would send 6,000 men, supported by a fleet, to help Louis fighting in the Spanish Netherlands, in return for which he would receive Dunkirk and Mardyck when they fell into French hands. Mardyck fell on the 3rd October and was occupied by Sir John Reynolds whose place as commander of English troops was taken by Sir William Lockhart, when, shortly afterwards, he was lost at sea. On the 14th June 1658 the Battle of the Dunes took place near Dunkirk when Turenne attacked the Spanish. Lockhart's regiment took part in the action, attacking uphill against a superior Spanish force which they drove off, resulting in a total victory for the French and their Commonwealth allies.

*   *   *

Cromwell's second Parliament met in January 1658, by which time the Upper House had been appointed. This body, unlike the one it replaced, contained few peers and a vast preponderance of military men. In the Lower House, however, elections had permitted the return of previously excluded members after they had taken a mild oath not to act against the Protectorate. These members set about obstructing the workings of the House so that the split between Upper and Lower Houses quickly became so wide that on the 4th February both Houses were dissolved.

The Army was Cromwell's one permanent means of enforcing the law, but within that large body dissention was already

154

rife thanks to the propaganda distributed by extremists such as the Levellers and Fifth Monarchists. Fears that Cromwell would become King in name as well as deed had heightened hostility, but when the Protector refused the title he pacified a large section of the Army. There was, moreover, little love lost between the Parliament and the Army for the power of the former was largely eroded by the presence of the latter. Parliament sought to diminish the Army and interfere with its running to such an extent that it was chiefly this reason which caused Cromwell to dissolve his final Parliament. The Army reaffirmed its loyalty and support to the Protector on the 6th February 1658 but at the same time Cromwell was forced to purge his own Regiment of horse of republicans, including the regimental commander, Major William Packer, who was cashiered.

*   *   *

Cromwell had aged quickly during his years as Protector and the loss of his daughter, Elizabeth Claypole, on the 6th August came as a blow to him. For a month he ailed although he tried to shrug the indisposition off but on the 3rd September he died.

He was succeeded by his son, Richard, who was incapable of leading the country with the necessary firmness. The Parliament immediately set about the destruction of those institutions it most abhored – chiefly the Army. The Republicans were more open in their attacks although the moderate voices were also heard. The Army, incensed by this, requested their arrears of pay, and announced their readiness otherwise to purge the House of 'wicked' Members. On the 22nd April 1659 Fleetwood brought about the dissolution of the House by a show of force, leaving the Council of Officers once more in control of the country. It was decided to resurrect the Long Parliament and this long-dead body assembled at Westminster in May, one

155

George Monck

of its first acts being another attempt to curb the power of the Army. Fleetwood was appointed General, but his command was only for a limited time and furthermore, officers commission were supposed to be signed by the Speaker. The Army disliked this turn of events, but another Royalist uprising prevented any immediate action being taken. The Rising, intended to be made throughout the country, was once again discovered by Thurloe. Lord Willoughby of Parham was to seize Lynn, Massey to take Gloucester, several other Royalists, Shrewsbury and the ever vigilant western Royalists, Cornwall and Devon. Massey's plot was discovered and he himself was captured although he later managed to escape. In the North, Sir George Booth seized Chester – the only success of this Rising. Together with Middleton he marched out to meet Lambert who was sent to crush the rebellion. The Royalists were routed after a short fight at Winnington Bridge and Chester fell the following day.

156

Death mask of Oliver Cromwell

Booth was captured and put in the Tower. The swift and crushing defeat put paid to the King's plan of invading England, while the successful ending of the Rising enabled the Army and Parliament to concentrate once again on their own quarrel. Fleetwood's commission was cancelled and the command of the Army was placed in the hands of seven commissioners. Eight officers, including Lambert, were then cashiered. The army acted promptly; Lambert marched musketeers to Westminster Hall and effectively ended yet another Parliament, returning power once more to the Council of Officers. This body set up a Committee of Safety to administer the country until a new constitution was devised, but by the time this happened, in February 1660, the country was largely against the Council and even the Army was not united behind it. Late in 1659, Monck had threatened to march on London unless the Long Parliament was reinstated. This proved to be unnecessary for so many Army garrisons declared for Parliament that the Council was forced to restore the Long Parliament on the 26th December, two months before the next Parliament was due.

Monck arrived in London in February to be appointed Commander-in-Chief of the Army. After complying with Parliament's requests, which included readmitting members excluded in 1648, he requested it to dissolve itself. Provision was made for elections and Parliament duly dissolved on the 16th March. The elections returned a majority of Royalists and moderate Presbyterians who met on the 25th April with the House of Lords also restored.

It was by now fairly evident that Monck was negotiating for the restoration of the House of Stuart and although the Army was generally hostile to this idea, there was little it could do because it was too disunited for any alternative action. Lambert, who had tried to prevent Monck's southward march in February and had been put in the Tower for his pains, escaped and raised a small force in Northamptonshire in April, but most of his men deserted and Lambert was put back in the Tower.

The newly elected Parliament at once began to negotiate with Charles who, on the 4th April, had issued the Delcaration of Breda. This document provided for an indemnity to all but those exempted by Parliament, *'liberty to tender consciences,'* settlement of the land question confused by the sequestration of the Commonwealth and of course reimbursement of arrears of army pay. On the 8th May Charles was proclaimed King and on the 25th May he landed at Dover.

The King was ecstatically received everywhere. It was eleven years since the death of Charles I and in that time the English had had their fill of the utopian Commonwealth with which the Civil Wars had left them. The country was, as a whole, happy to have a King once more in Whitehall.

Bibliography

The King's War – C.V. Wedgewood 1958
The King's Peace – C.V. Wedgewood
Hastings to Culloden – Peter Young & J. Adair 1964
Battles of the Civil War – Peter Young & J. Adair 1961
The Great Civil War – A. Woolrych 1959
Cromwell, Our Chief of Men – Antonia Fraser
Oliver Cromwell – Peter Young 1962
The Battlefields of England – A.H. Burne 1951
Battlefields of Europe – David Chandler 1965

Index

161

162

Lindsey, Lord 48, 60
Liskeard 63
longbow 30
'Long' Parliament 17, 145
London 50, 51, 55, 60, 61, 63, 73, 74, 124
Lostwithiel 93, 95
Lucas, Sir Charles 124, 130
Lyme Regis 73, 82, 84

Maidstone 122–123
Mandeville, Lord 21
Marlborough 62
Massey, Col. Edward 73, 141, 142, 144, 156
Marston Moor 42, 91–93, 96
matchlock muskets 36
Maurice, Prince 51, 66, 68, 70, 71, 76, 82, 111
Meldrum, Sir John 80–81, 91
Meon, East and West 78
Merrick, Sir John 49
Middleton, John 85
Middleton, Sir Thomas 111, 128, 140, 144
Militia Bill 20
Monck, George 8, 135, 138, 144
musket, musketeers, 31, 33, 36, 37, 41, 44
Muskham Bridge 81

Nantwich 82
Naseby 109
National Covenant (1638) 16
Neale, Sir William 81
Newark 80
Newbridge 83
Newbury, 35, 74, 98, 99
Newcastle, Earl of 82, 83
New Model Army 40, 41, 46, 101, 107, 108, 109, 115, 120, 122, 132, 135, 151
Newport Pagnell 108
Northampton, Earl of 66, 85
Nottingham 51

Okehampton 64
Oxford 60, 62, 63, 66, 68, 70, 71, 80, 83, 107, 108, 118

Pembroke Castle 121
Pendennis Castle 117, 118
Penruddock, Col. John 150
Percy, Harry 100
Pershore 74
Peterborough, Earl of 49
pike, pikemen 30, 31, 32, 37–38, 41, 44
Plymouth 62, 64
Porter, George 112
Portsmouth 54
Postcombe 68
Powick, Bridge 54–55, 143
Pym, John 17, 21, 22, 24

Raglan Castle 118
Ramsey, Sir James 58
Reading 60, 62, 66, 68, 80
Rigby, Col. Alexander 87
Ripple 66
Roche, Bartholomew de la 51
Rochester 150
Root and Branch Bill (1641) 18
Rupert, Prince 43, 48, 51–54, 60–61, 67, 71–72, 73, 75–76, 80–83, 87–88, 90–92, 96, 102, 107–109, 114–116
Ruthin, General 63
Ruthven, Patrick 48, 57

Saltash 64
Sandys, Col. Edwin 55
Seacroft Moor 76
Severn Valley 66
Ship Money 15, 18
'Short' Parliament 17
Shrewsbury 80, 102, 104
Sion House 61
Skippon, Philip 27, 49, 50, 109, 124
Slanning, Sir Nicholas 62
Slingsby, Col. Walter 69
Somerset 62, 66
Stamford, Earl of 64
Stow-in-the-Wold 73, 117
Stratton 66
Strode, William 21
Stuart, Lord Bernard 85
Sudeley Castle 84
Swords 39

Tadcaster 91
Taunton 111
'tercio' formation 31–32
Tewkesbury 74

Thame 68
Tichborne 80
Tillier, Col. Henry 81, 92
Trained Bands 27–29, 61, 63–64,
  73–74, 120, 124
Trevannion, Col. John 62
Triennial Act 18
trooper 39
Tunnage and Poundage 10, 21
Turnham Green 61

Urry, Col. John 68

Venn, Col. John 61
Verney, Sir Edmund 24, 60
Villiers, Lord Francis 125

Wagstaffe, Sir Joseph 149–150

Waller, Sir William 25, 66, 68–69, 72,
  76, 77–78, 83–86, 93, 96, 98
Warwick 56, 74
Warwick, Earl of 22
Washington, Col. Henry 72
Wedgewood C.V. 10–11
Wentworth, Thomas, Earl of Strafford
  9, 17–18, 117
Western Association 66
Wexford 8
Winceby 76
Winchester 80, 117
Windsor Castle 61
Wilmot, Lord Henry (later Earl of
  Rochester) 48, 58, 62, 70, 73, 100,
  149
Worcester 8, 54, 56, 66, 84, 142–143

York 50, 68, 95

164